The Swords and the Sorrows

THE SWORDS AND THE SORROWS CLAIDHEAMHAN IS BRÓN

AN EXHIBITION TO COMMEMORATE THE JACOBITE RISING OF 1745 AND THE BATTLE OF CULLODEN 1746

16 APRIL – 20 SEPTEMBER 1996

The Swords and the Sorrows

The exhibition *The Swords and the Sorrows* was held at the Visitor Centre on Drumossie Moor from 16 April to 20 September 1996, to mark the Jacobite Rising of 1745 and Battle of Culloden in 1746. We would particularly like to thank Geoffrey Jenkinson for suggesting the exhibition of commemoration and for lending his finest swords.
The exhibition gathered together many battle-related objects with a connection with the '45. Most are of the period or earlier, the majority were of Scottish workmanship of the highest quality and as far as possible had not been exhibited before.
April 16 was the date of the battle and 20 September the date that Prince Charles left Scotland.

The exhibition was organised by John Batty, Assistant Curator, The National Trust for Scotland.
Exhibition and catalogue designed by Ian Boyter, Chief Designer, The National Trust for Scotland.

Acknowledgements

The National Trust for Scotland wishes to thank the following for all their help in making the exhibition and catalogue possible:

Her Majesty the Queen

Miss C W H Aikman; The Earl of Airlie; Albavision Ltd; The Duke of Argyll; Ashmolean Museum; The Duke of Atholl; Maj David Back; Sir Geoffrey de Bellaigue; Claude Blair; Mr & Mrs Norman Blank; Bookspeed; Ninian Brodie of Brodie; Anne S K Brown Military Collection; Anthony Bryant; The Duke of Buccleuch & Queensberry KT; Pam Buchanan; Anne Buddle; Cabrach Whisky Company; Caldon Contracts; Dr David Caldwell, Lt Col Sir Donald Cameron of Lochiel; Margaret Cameron; Alastair Campbell of Airds; Annie Campbell; Hugh Cheape; Krista Chisholm; Christie's Images; City of Dundee District Council Art Galleries & Museums; Rosalyn Clancey; Mike Clarkson; Timothy Clifford; Ann Clipson; Mr & Mrs W Corey; Rosie Croll; The Culloden Advisory Committee; Culloden Highland Games & Scottish Festival, USA; Drambuie Ltd; Mrs Blanche Ellis; Exclusive Card Company; Capt A C Farquharson of Invercauld; Peter Finer; Forth Photography; Fortrose Women's Guild; Gordon Foster; Provost W A E Fraser; Rodney French; Edward Fuller; Ranald Gayre; General Accident Insurance; Alex Gillespie; Glasgow Museums and Art Galleries; Mrs Ann Gloag; Peggie Gordon; Brian Grainge; Ian Grant of Glenmoriston; R T Gwynn; Peter Harrington; Christopher Hartley; Peter Hartley; Peter Hawkins; David Heron; Highland Members' Centre; James Holloway; Hilary Horrocks; Deborah Hunter; Julian D H Hutchings; I F Construction; Innes & Cromb Ltd; Inverness Courier; Victor James; Geoffrey Jenkinson; Susanna Kerr; Kiltarlity SWRI; John Kirk; G Kong, Dickens Restaurant; Philip J Lankester; Myra Lawson; David Learmont; Stephen Lloyd; MacAllan-Glenlivet; MacAndrew & Jenkins; N McCann; Ross MacKenzie; Bruce Mackie; Mackintosh of Mackintosh; David MacLearie; William Marshall; Katharine Mitchell; Jackie Moran; Janice Murray; The Museum and Galleries Commission; Nairn District Council; National Museums of Scotland; Diana Keith Neal; The Trustees of The William Keith Neal Foundation; Charlotte Neilson; Robin Nicholson; Brian Noads; A V B Norman; Caroline Paybody; The Pilgrim Press; Antonia Reeve; Adam Ritchie; Isla Robertson; Eric Rooney; The Royal Museum of Scotland; Scottish National Portrait Gallery; Scottish United Services Museum; John Sheerin; Shetland Jewellery; Souter & Jaffrey; Diana Stevens; Alexander Stewart of Ardvorlich; Stirling Gallery Publications; Stirling Hendry & Co; Margaret Swain; Textile Heritage Collection; Christopher Thornton; Fraser Tidy; Angela Town; Upper Strathglass WRI; Mr and Mrs J St A Warde; John Watson; The Earl of Wemyss & March; David Wemyss of Wemyss; Westair Productions Ltd; David Williams; Lady Jane Willoughby de Eresby; Dick Wilson; Stephen Wood; Veronica Woodman; Robert C Woosnam-Savage; Worldwide TV News.

Special thanks are due to The National Trust for Scotland Highland Members' Centre, who initiated the local appeal with a generous donation.

ISBN 0 901625 58 2

Published by The National Trust for Scotland Trading Company Ltd, 1996.

Photographs by Forth Photography.
Origination and printing by J Thomson Colour Printers Ltd, Glasgow.
Printed on Consort Royal Silk Tint, s/o 135gsm manufactured by Donside Paper Co, Aberdeen.

Contents

Full details of references in text and footnotes appear in the Bibliography.

Notes on contributors

***Ross Mackenzie** is Property Manager at The National Trust for Scotland's Visitor Centre at Culloden.*

***Hugh Cheape** is Assistant Keeper, The National Museums of Scotland. He is Curator of the Scottish Collections spanning the seventeenth to twentieth centuries.*

***A V B Norman**, former Inspector of Armouries at the Wallace Collection and Master of Armouries at the Tower of London, is recognised as a leading authority on edged weapons. He has written extensively on arms and armour. Without his help, this catalogue could not have been written.*

***John Batty** has been Assistant Curator, The National Trust for Scotland since 1971. As exhibition organiser, he has gathered the exhibits together and written many catalogue entries.*

***Jackie Moran** is Museum Assistant at the Museum of Antiquities, Edinburgh.*

***Gordon Foster** is Head of Silver at Christie's, Scotland.*

***James Holloway** is Assistant Keeper, Scottish National Portrait Gallery.*

Foreword

The origins of Jacobitism and the course of the '45

By Ross Mackenzie

If the original plans of the Jacobites and their French allies had come to fruition, the '45 would have been the '44.

It was in that year that the French, on the defensive in the War of the Austrian Succession, had decided to open a second front against their British and Austrian enemies, using the Jacobite threat against the recently established, and still unpopular, Hanoverian monarchy in Britain. To the exiled Jacobite court in Rome it meant another chance to regain the thrones of the three kingdoms – England, Ireland and Scotland – from which the Stuarts had been driven by the so-called 'Glorious Revolution' of 1688/89.

In 1688, James VII of Scotland and II of England and Ireland had been forced to flee the country in the face of a conspiracy by the disaffected English nobility, who feared that after the birth of an heir, James would attempt to impose Catholicism on the country. James's daughter Princess Mary and her husband William, Prince of Orange, were invited to assume the throne as the defenders of Protestant liberties. Without the presence of the king, royalist resistance in England speedily collapsed. William and Mary acceded to the throne on 24 December, 1688, after the legal fiction of James's resignation had been accepted by the peers in London, and William had been invited to assume the executive functions of government. In Scotland and Ireland, however, matters had taken a different course.

The Scottish parliament contained many supporters of James (he was after all the descendant of the ancient Scottish royal line), and many others who were waiting to see how the wind blew. Edinburgh Castle, commanding the capital, was held for James by the Duke of Gordon, and James Graham of Claverhouse, Viscount Dundee, actively promoted the king's cause. James, badly advised as ever in Scottish affairs by his Secretary of State, the Earl of Melfort, alienated the Scottish parliament, whilst William won over many waverers by a carefully worded letter promising much, but in the end delivering little. The Edinburgh parliament offered the throne of Scotland to William and Mary: Dundee left to fight for the king.

A MINIATURE OF PRINCE CHARLES EDWARD STUART BY AN UNKNOWN ARTIST

Avoiding arrest by forces loyal to the new regime, Dundee raised an army of royalists to win back for James at least the throne of Scotland. His troops marched south from Lochaber in May 1689 and reached Blair Atholl by 26 July, intending to hold it against a government force commanded by Major-General Hugh Mackay. Mackay, camped at Dunkeld, moved his men against Dundee on the 27th, through the narrow gorge of Killiecrankie. As they emerged from the pass, Dundee's army of some 2,000 men fell on them and utterly routed them – but Dundee himself was mortally wounded, and with his death the royal cause in Scotland suffered a setback from which it was never to recover. In Ireland, with James himself in command, it was to last for another two years, but with the defeat of his troops at the Boyne in 1690 and again at Aughrim in 1691, many Jacobites retreated to France to regroup.

James VII and II died on 6 September, 1701. Louis XIV of France, enmeshed in a bitter war with William of Orange, immediately recognised his son as James VIII and III. William himself died on 8 March 1702, and James VII and II's younger daughter Anne, another Protestant, took the throne. History was to know James's son as the 'Old Pretender', and there were another three abortive attempts to win back his ancestral crowns – in 1708, 1715, and 1719 – before he personally gave up hope.

THE BATTLE OF KILLIECRANKIE (ILLUSTRATION BY ALLAN HERIOT)

British Jacobites, however, never gave up hope. With the death of Anne in 1714, Britain saw the last of the Stuart monarchs, and the throne devolved to George, Elector of Hanover, a Protestant; James, the 'Old Pretender' and his line were passed over as Catholics by the terms of the English parliament's Act of Settlement of 1701. In this situation, it was imperative that the Stuart line should continue. In 1719, James married the Polish princess Marie Clementina Sobieska and just over a year later, in December 1720, an heir was born to James in Rome – Prince Charles Edward Louis John Casimir Silvester Severino Maria Stuart. He was to be better known as the 'Young Pretender', or 'Bonnie Prince Charlie' – the man who was to come so close to restoring the Stuarts in 1745.

Charles was brought up to believe in the justice of his father's cause, and of his own rights as Prince of Wales. He was an attractive and intelligent child (despite his atrocious spelling), and easily won over the Italians with his prowess as a sportsman and hunter. At the age of 14 Charles participated in the siege by Spain of the Italian town of Gaeta and won high praise from his cousin the Duke of Liria, commander of the Spanish armies. Gaeta was a propaganda triumph for Charles, who was considered to have the makings of a great general.

The Stuarts, exiled in St Germain, then Avignon, and finally Rome, were never able to contemplate the attempt on Britain without assistance from one of the great European powers opposed to the House of Hanover. It was their misfortune that whenever prospects in Britain favoured them, prospects in Europe did not, and their requests for assistance were politely but firmly refused. On the other hand, when it suited a European power it would attempt to use the Jacobites for its own ends, as did Spain in the Rising of 1719, regardless of any other considerations. Jacobitism found itself trapped by the European power politics of the day. Popular support there was aplenty, but given the nature of early modern Britain, without military aid it was impossible to win and hold the country. There were parliamentary elections, but with so circumscribed and corrupt an electorate, change could only be achieved through military means – a fact that many modern critics of the Jacobites fail to recognise.

At last, in 1743, fate seemed to favour the cause. France – engaged in a war with Britain and Austria and fought to a standstill in the Low Countries – sought to open a second front. Now the Jacobites could play their part in French plans, and at the same time win what they most desired, the three thrones of Britain.

The Marechal de Saxe, France's leading soldier, prepared his forces for a landing on the south coast of England in February of 1744. Letters were sent out to leading Jacobites to prepare them for the invasion and ensure support on landing. Charles Edward arrived in the Channel port of Gravelines in late February 1744, ready to play his part. All seemed set fair – all, that is, except the weather. Storms destroyed most of Saxe's fleet, and the French government decided that their best option lay elsewhere. The invasion of Britain was cancelled, much to Charles's fury. He had come far, only to be stopped by a storm. He remained in France as an increasingly embarrassing guest of a government which, following the cancellation of the invasion, had no idea what to do with him and suggested that he go back to Rome. Charles, however, had not come so far to be turned back. He decided to see what

Prince Charles Edward Stuart landing in Scotland (illustration by Jim Proudfoot)

could be done without official support. With the help of émigré Scots, such as Antoine Walsh and Aeneas MacDonald, the Prince was able to equip two ships, the Du Teillay *and the* Elisabeth, *with men and arms, and sailed from Nantes for Scotland on 12 July 1745. The two ships were spotted by the Royal Navy ship HMS* Lion *on 20 July and, after a savage sea battle, the* Elisabeth *had to put back to port in France with many casualties and all Charles Edward's arms and munitions. The* Du Teillay *continued on to Scotland. Charles landed on Eriskay on 23 July; all he had were seven companions and an indomitable will with which to raise a nation for his father. It is a measure of his genius that he so nearly succeeded.*

From Eriskay, Charles made for the mainland to raise the clans there, despite having been given the news that the MacLeods and the MacDonalds of Sleat had refused to rise. The Prince's ship put into Loch nan Uamh on 25 July, and anchored at Lochailort in Arisaig. Here the first Highland supporters began to arrive – young Clanranald, MacDonald of Glenaladale and Kinlochmoidart – and letters announcing the Prince's arrival were sent out to Jacobite supporters. Further attempts were made to raise the MacLeods and Sleat MacDonalds, but to no avail; more important for the Prince was the decision of Cameron of Locheil to come out. After much hesitation, Locheil was persuaded to join the Rising during a personal interview with the Prince; his support was the turning point. Without it, it is likely that the '45 would have petered out quickly; with it came more new recruits for the cause, and the Prince fixed 19 August as the day for raising the royal standard at Glenfinnan, confident that things were going his way.

The Raising of the Standard at Glenfinnan (illustration by C E Collingwood)

From Glenfinnan, Charles's small army, numbering at this time some 1,200 men, moved south. They knew that General Cope, the government commander in Scotland, had moved north to intercept them and prepared for battle. The Jacobite army reached the head of the Corryairack Pass first and waited for Cope to arrive. Realising that the Pass was held against him, Cope feared an ambush, and made for Inverness with his troops. The road to the south was open, with no government troops available to stop the Jacobite army as it marched south. Perth fell to the Prince on 4 September, and here he stayed for a week, as new supporters came in – Lord Nairne, Lord Ogilvy, the Duke of Perth and Lord George Murray, perhaps the single most important recruit of the whole campaign. From Perth the army headed south for Edinburgh, bypassing Stirling and its castle, and reached the capital by 16 September. Negotiations were opened for surrender with the burgh council, who feared bloodshed if the city held out against Charles's troops. After inconclusive talks, the Edinburgh deputation returned to the city by way of the Netherbow port, which was left open just long enough for a party of Jacobite troops to seize it and enter the city. Edinburgh, the capital of Scotland, had fallen without a shot being fired, and the jubilant Jacobite army made themselves masters of the city. The castle, however, remained in government hands and was to prove troublesome to the Jacobites. Charles Edward held court at the Palace of Holyroodhouse and the London government at last realised just how serious the rising in Scotland was.

In the meantime Cope had had his men shipped south from Aberdeen, and they landed at Dunbar on 16 September. It was clear that battle would be joined soon and the Jacobite army prepared for it. Cope marched from Dunbar to camp at Prestonpans; here the Jacobite army fell on them and utterly routed a force of seasoned government troops, killing some 500 out of a force of 2,600, and losing only 25 out of 2,400 men. Support continued to flow in, from the traditional Jacobite heartlands of Angus, Perthshire, Aberdeen and Moray and, at last, from France. Louis XV's government realised its opportunity to draw away British troops from the Continent, and sent money and supplies which began landing at the east coast ports of Montrose and Stonehaven. News was also coming in of the government's reaction, with troops sent north and regiments recalled from Flanders to help deal with the rising. All over England, defences were being strengthened and a counter-attack was being prepared. Charles Edward decided to strike first, and on 31 October his army marched out of Edinburgh to invade England, heading for London.

The Jacobites marched south, taking Carlisle, Penrith, Preston, Manchester, Macclesfield and then Derby. The speed with which Charles's men marched outpaced the lumbering government regiments, and they were in the heart of England before the government was aware of it. The news that the Jacobite army had reached Derby caused panic in London, with a run on the Bank of England, and it is said that George II had the royal yacht prepared to flee the country. But all was not well in the Jacobite army. Charles's commanders were worried that their supply lines were too long; that no English Jacobites, other than the Manchester Regiment, had joined them; that there was no sign of promised French support and that they were about to be caught in a trap surrounded by three government armies. The vote to retreat went against Charles, who insisted that if the army pressed on the country would be theirs once London fell. To his dying day he considered that the wrong

Illustrations of Prince Charles Edward Stuart and The Duke of Cumberland by Jim Proudfoot

decision had been taken at Derby. The Jacobite army began the retreat to Scotland on 'Black Friday', 6 December 1745. The London government could not believe its luck.

A government army under George II's younger and favourite son, William Augustus, the Duke of Cumberland, shadowed the Jacobite army northwards, but apart from a brief skirmish at Clifton, the greater speed of the Jacobites kept the two forces well apart, and they reached Scotland safely on 20 December 1745. The Jacobite army headed for Glasgow, a city with Whig sympathies and not at all supportive of Charles, where they stayed for a week, levying supplies and money from the openly hostile burghers. From Glasgow the army moved on towards Stirling to besiege the town and castle. The town fell quickly, but the castle held out and tied up men and supplies in a worthless siege.

Whilst the Jacobite army had been in England, government forces had retaken Edinburgh: General Hawley had been appointed their commander. Despising the Jacobite army as a worthless rabble, he moved out of Edinburgh, seeking to engage them in battle and end the rising once and for all. On 17 January the two armies came upon each other at Falkirk where, once again, the Jacobites routed a government army of seasoned troops, forcing Hawley to flee back to Edinburgh. The failing light of a January afternoon and confused orders prevented the Jacobites from following up their victory, but the battle showed them still to be a dangerous foe. Recruits were still coming in – Lord Lewis Gordon had raised a second Jacobite army in the north-east, and clans such as the Frasers and Mackenzies joined the army. The government forces still had much to overcome before the Rising was defeated.

After Falkirk, Cumberland moved his main force to Edinburgh, where he built up supplies and concentrated on training his men for the forthcoming battle. The Jacobites had given up the siege of Stirling, and Charles Edward had been forced to order a retreat of the army north, into the Highlands, where his commanders felt that it would be better able to fight Cumberland. The army split in two, with Charles and the Highland regiments heading north by way of Blair Atholl and Dalwhinnie; Lord George Murray took the Lowland regiments and cavalry north via Montrose and Aberdeen. Both made for Inverness, which was in the hands of government troops under Lord Loudoun – the Jacobite army's next objective.

The Prince reached Moy Hall, seat of the Mackintoshes, on 16 February, where he was entertained by the fiercely pro-Jacobite Lady Anne Mackintosh. Loudoun, hearing of this and knowing that the Prince had only a small bodyguard with him, attempted a surprise attack. Gathering his men, he sealed off Inverness to prevent word reaching the Prince, and marched the 16 miles to Moy. Unfortunately for him, word had got out: the Prince was bundled out into the hills on a freezing February night, and five local men, led by Donald Fraser the local blacksmith, fired off guns and shouted clan slogans to make Loudoun believe that he had stumbled on the entire Jacobite army. Loudoun's 1,500-strong force retreated in what became known as the 'Rout of Moy'. Charles Edward, following up his advantage, gathered together 2,000 of his men and attacked Inverness. Loudoun fled, and lost many men in confused skirmishing around the town. Inverness now became the main Jacobite base for the remainder of the campaign. Lord George Murray reached there on 19 February, and Inverness Castle capitulated.

Cumberland had finally moved out of Edinburgh, following the Jacobite army north by the east coast route. He reached Aberdeen on 27 February, and stayed until 8 April, training his men and building up sufficient supplies for the march to Inverness through hostile country. With Cumberland remaining in Aberdeen, the Jacobites took the war to the government: a series of operations showed they were as dangerous as ever and their victories heightened morale. Fort Augustus was besieged and fell after two days; Fort William was surrounded, but here the siege dragged on; Loudoun and his remaining forces, a threat since the taking of Inverness, were routed by the Duke of Perth and fled to Skye; Lord George Murray surrounded and captured without loss, 30 government blockhouses protecting the approaches to Blair Castle. March 1746 saw the zenith of Jacobite military success. April was to see its nadir.

Despite their successes, money and supplies for the Jacobite army were short. Cumberland, on the other hand, had made painstaking preparations and had ensured that his army was fully supplied. One army would fight at Culloden hungry and weary, the other with full bellies. On 8 April 1746, Cumberland and his army moved out of Aberdeen heading straight for the Jacobite heart, Inverness. On 14 April they camped at Nairn, preparing for battle. Charles Edward faced the prospect of battle lacking half his army – they were scattered across the north attacking government troops, or looking for food. Out of a total possible strength of 9,000, Charles faced his enemy with 4,500 men. Cumberland had over 9,000.

Charles Edward was convinced that Cumberland would give battle on 15 April, his birthday, and had his army drawn up on the moor above Culloden House to wait for him. But Cumberland remained at Nairn, and Charles's troops stood on the moor all day, with nothing but a biscuit to eat. Charles then decided on a surprise attack on Cumberland's camp, reasoning that his men would have celebrated his birthday and be too drunk to defend themselves. But his army had already started to drift back to Inverness in search of food, and by the time enough were collected for the attack, it was already too late. It went ahead, nevertheless, and the Jacobites approached the camp at Nairn just as it was wakening; having lost the element of surprise they had no option but to retrace their steps to Culloden. Here they slumped exhausted, many not wakening until the government troops were upon them and killing them.

Culloden Moor was the Prince's choice of field, advised by O'Sullivan, one of the 'Seven Men of Moidart'. It was the wrong place to fight Cumberland, given the Jacobite army's tactics and lack of artillery, but because the Prince had never forgiven Lord George Murray for forcing the retreat from Derby, he ignored his better advice. Cumberland, learning of the failure of the night attack, mobilised his men. By eleven o'clock in the morning of 16 April, the two armies were in sight of each other. Cumberland's army advanced in good order, whilst the Jacobite army, still tired from the night march and foraging for food, had to be hurriedly gathered together to face their foes.

The battle was over in less than an hour. Cumberland's superior artillery saw off the Jacobite guns and tore huge gaps in the Jacobite ranks before Charles Edward gave the order to charge. His right wing reached the government army and did some damage before being forced to retreat, but the Jacobite left was shot apart and retreated. Flank attacks by Cumberland's cavalry broke the shattered Jacobite army, and a general retreat began. Charles Edward lost between 1,200 and 1,500 men; Cumberland only 50. Charles was led off the field to begin his six months in the heather, before escaping to France. Some 4,000 survivors of Culloden and fresh Jacobite troops assembled at Ruthven in Badenoch waiting for orders to carry on the struggle – but they never came. Charles, the fight gone out of him, ordered them to disperse, to find whatever mercy they could from the victorious government forces. The '45 was over and the 'ethnic cleansing' of the Highlands could begin.

Broadsword Charge on 'Brown Bess' (illustration by C E Collingwood)

The story of the '45 is a complex one. It begins in 1688 with a royal deposition, and ends in 1746 on Culloden Moor with slaughter. It is easy to see Culloden as the final result in an England v Scotland, or Catholic v Protestant contest – but it was much more than that. There were Scots on both sides, just as there were English on both sides; the large Episcopalian element in Charles's army had more in common with the Anglicans of Cumberland's army than they did with the Presbyterian Campbells, also in the government army, but that did not save them in the atrocities after the battle. The terrible punishment for treason in the eighteenth century meant that those who came out for the Jacobite cause did not do so lightly, and shows the high level of commitment to the Stuart cause that over fifty years of foreign exile could not destroy. Also, the '45 should not be viewed as a singularly British affair – it was part of the greater European conflict of the War of the Austrian Succession, in which politicians from all the countries involved sought to use the Stuarts for their own advantage. It was Scotland's tragedy to be caught in the middle of a power struggle over which she had no control and which ultimately cost her dear.

Preface

Highland and Jacobite Culture

By Hugh Cheape

Alastair Grant the Champion: painting by Richard Waitt

The stereotype image of the Jacobite supporter in the '45 Rising is of the kilted Highlander, the Gael from Scotland's mountainous north and west. But support for the exiled Stuarts in the short term, and also in the long term of what has been called the 'Jacobite Century' from the Revolution to the death of Prince Charles Edward, was more complex and more widespread. Scots (and English) actively or passively supported the Stuarts because of religious sympathies as Episcopalians and Roman Catholics, political scruples against the Union of 1707 and the Hanoverian Succession, or a more fundamental belief in the inalienable and divinely ordained right of the Stuarts to retain the throne of the United Kingdom.

Regard for the old monarchy remained particularly high in Scotland whose ancient race of kings they were, and was expressed forcibly and in equal terms in the late seventeenth and eighteenth centuries as it had been as an article of faith in the Declaration of Arbroath in 1320: 'This Kingdom has been governed by an uninterrupted succession of 113 kings, all of our own native and royal stock without the intervening of any stranger'.

Support for the Stuarts was evident nationally in Scotland although scholarly opinion has varied on how real or effective this was. In terms of men under arms in 1745 more Scots probably enlisted against the Stuarts than with them. Three Scottish regiments fought at Culloden, the 1st, 21st and 25th of Foot, and volunteers and militia companies accounted for large numbers of men, such as most notably the Argyll Militia (2,776 by March 1746), the Earl of Loudon's Companies (c2,000), and the militia corps of Glasgow and Edinburgh. In the Highlands and Islands, several of the great clans refused to join the Rising, such as the Campbells, the MacDonalds of Sleat, the MacLeods and the Grants, and many Highlanders and Hebrideans served in the government's militia companies. In spite of these discrepancies and a large proportion of Lowland support, especially from the Episcopalian districts of the North East, the strength of the Jacobite army in 1745 was in its Highland contingents and the image of the tartan-clad Highlander is an accurate if superficial measure of Jacobite culture.

The image of the tartan-clad Highlander is also a measure of Highland culture more generally but it applies with certain qualifications: in the first place, it is not a timeless image stretching back into prehistory but probably emerges only in the late fifteenth or sixteenth centuries. Secondly, tartan was not the dress of everyone going about their daily business: it was more a dress of fashion and social exclusiveness, and worn more usually away from home than in it. Finally, it was not a clan badge or uniform but was designed and woven according to preferences for different colours (often varying from district to district) or availability of dyestuffs. In a significant note in his account of the campaign of 1745, the great Gaelic poet, Alexander MacDonald of Dalilea in Moidart, described how:

'We MacDonalds were much perplexed in the event of ane ingagement how to distinguish ourselves from our bretheren and nighbours the MacDonalds of Skye, seeing we were both Highlanders and both wore heather in our bonnets, only our white cockades made some distinction'.

The defeat of the Jacobite army on the battlefield of Culloden in 1746 marked the beginning of the end of the Highland and Gaelic way of life. The British government, with legislation, strategic measures such as road and fortress building, and with an army of occupation, was making deliberate efforts to break up Gaelic society. The campaign of attrition which began on 16 April 1746 was a measure of their determination to destroy the military and political threat which the Highlands could mount and also a strategy to pre-empt the renewed outbreak of hostilities then seen as a real threat. This was a devastating blow to Highland culture but not the first and not the last. Confrontation between Highlands and Lowlands, between an established government and Gaelic society, dates back to the fifteenth century.

Gaelic culture was predominant north of the Highland Line until the early eighteenth century

Much of what we now recognise as Highland or Gaelic culture emerged historically in two phases, in the late medieval period up to c1500 and in the ensuing sixteenth and seventeenth centuries. The earlier phase belongs to the so-called 'Lordship of the Isles' and the second phase is marked by the political, economic, military and social consequences of its destruction. The Lordship was a powerful political and strategic entity, virtually a kingdom within a kingdom, which established itself in the face of a Norse overlordship of the Northern and Western Isles and following the disappearance of Norse rule in the fourteenth century.

Families and communities in the Gaelic west placed themselves under the rule of strong leaders who could protect them and win lands from the Vikings. Descended from the Gaelic tribes and leaders who had occupied Scotland from Ireland up to and after the sixth century, they fought to regain the territories of Dal Riada which they believed belonged to them. Pre-eminent among such kings or leaders was Somerled, twelfth-century ruler of Argyll, and his descendants of Clan Donald. All MacDonalds trace their descent from Domhnall mac Raonaill 'ic Somhairle, *Donald son of Ranald son of Somerled, and Donald's grandson was John of Islay, who assumed the title 'Lord of the Isles'. The Hebrides under the Lords of the Isles and emerging from Norse rule became a strong focus for Gaelic culture. Consistently and over a long period, the arts of learning and language, music and song, and the crafts of sculpture and metalwork were encouraged by successive leaders of Clan Donald.*

The forfeiture of the Lordship of the Isles in the 1490s was a decisive gesture by Scotland's Renaissance monarch, James IV. The kings of Scots had been severely tested by this powerful Gaelic principality asserting its independence within Scotland (even making treaties with the kings of England) and its close association with Gaelic society in Ireland, not only in political and military alliances but also in the practice and maintenance of the arts of learning and music. Specific and determined attempts had been made sporadically since the twelfth century to bring the Highlands and Islands under the control of the Crown and an increasingly centralised kingship of the Scots. Sanctions imposed by royal policy were parried by the Gaels or negotiated and accepted because the Stuart kings shared their descent and were accorded for the most part the loyalty which earlier had been reserved for their own princes.

James VI's words in Basilicon Doron, *the 'Kingly Gift', have been quoted many times. They were written by him for his eldest son, Prince Henry, in a book of instruction on the principles of statecraft and duties of a king. They are significant not so much as revealing an ongoing government policy against the unruly Highlands but as marking the beginning of a process of cultural attrition which was to continue unabated into the eighteenth century and beyond and in which the '45 Rising was the most fateful punctuation mark:*

'As for the Highlands, I shortly comprehend them all in two sorts of people: the one that dwelleth in our mainland, that are barbarous for the most part, and yet mixed with some show of civility: the other that dwelleth in the Isles, and are utterly barbarians, without any sort or show of civility ...'

These words advertise the determined attempts by the Crown, especially in the person of James VI and more especially after the Union of the Crowns in 1603, to bring the Highlands and Islands within the scope of Crown control. The Crown required to draw on fresh sources of wealth, real or imagined – and contemporary documents reveal a belief in the untapped resources of the Hebrides – but also to extend an effective direct rule over Highland society and to break its traditional links with Ireland.

Among a series of Acts of Parliament designed by the young King James to bring law and order to his realm was the law ordering chieftains and landholders to produce their charters and title deeds to the Lords of Exchequer before 15 May 1598. Using the excuse of a perceived 'barbarus inhumanitie', the measure was cunningly designed to place more land and its wealth at the disposal of the Crown. Those who failed to produce a title to land might lose their ancestral territories or more usually find that they were granted by feudal deed to a powerful but loyal subject. The feudal deed was generally an alien notion although one that had become increasingly familiar since the twelfth century. Those in possession naturally fought hard to retain their territories and the concept of lands 'held by the sword' was a familiar one.

This process of subinfeudation to Crown control following the collapse of the Lordship of the Isles was the cause of much of the clan warfare of the period and went far to mould the social and cultural characteristics of clanship with which history and literature has made us so familiar. The need for a 'following' for example became a very necessary device for holding on to clan lands, and the increasing need for manpower forced the chieftains in turn to

A 'black house' typical of a Highland community at the time of the '45 (illustration by Jim Proudfoot).

acquire land with which to reward and provide for their adherents. The need for more land lies behind nearly all the feuds of the period.

The other notable measure by James VI was the enforcement of sanctions on the Highlands and Islands. These were the 'Statutes of Iona' imposed on the Hebridean chieftains and subscribed by them in August 1609. Designed to reduce the political and strategic, as well as the cultural independence of the Gael, they initiated the process of hostile confrontation and serve to define Gaelic culture in terms of the outsiders' view. They ruled that moral standards, much under scrutiny since the Reformation, should be obeyed, that excessive drinking and traditions of hospitality should be curbed, that elder children should be sent to the Lowlands for their education 'quhill thay may be found able sufficientlie to speik, reid and wryte Inglische', and that the orders of poets should be banned. This latter stipulation may seem inconsequential but in contemporary terms, the bards were the political brains behind the military strength of the chieftains and the Crown and government were right to fear them.

It is almost a paradox of Scottish culture that has not been well explored that Britain and Europe were experiencing an era of civil and religious wars into which the Highlands and Islands as a whole and Gaelic culture were drawn. The role of the chief evolved to be political and military leader as well as patriarch, a cultural leader and provider of largesse, the focus and subject of poetry and song which rehearsed the feats of arms and traditions of the clan and its leaders. Many clansmen aspired to fight on behalf of their chieftain and his kin. Warfare involved set piece battles with small numbers of men on each side and the fighting of one battle was the whole art of war. Many of the clans depended on galleys for transport and deployment and such vessels, whether the larger long fhada *or 'lymphad' or smaller* birlinn, *could accommodate only small bodies of well-armed, picked men. Fighting was limited to a practised and hereditary warrior elite and training was directed to developing personal prowess. A battle was a charge, the tactically preferred charge downhill, followed by individual combat.*

Gaelic society honoured the warrior and consequently set store by the art of war as an aristocratic way of life. A high value was also placed on hunting while those who worked the land were held in low esteem. Conventional eulogy praised the warrior, the hunter, herdsman and the steersman, but never the farmer. A lament for a MacAulay chieftain of Uig in Lewis, a celebrated hunter of deer of the seventeenth century, includes the couplet:

'Cas a shiubhal nam fuar-bheann,
Ghabh thu roghainn bha uasal ...'
'Foot that travelled the cold mountain
You made the choice that was noble ...'

This ranking and driving force of values survived into the eighteenth century and can be seen in the military organisation of the clans during the '45. The Stewarts of Appin, strongly Jacobite in their affiliation, preserved the memory of the conventional formation of the clan regiment in battle. This formation, by 'order of nature', was strongly hierarchical and reflected the marked social ranking of Gaelic society. Every regiment or clan was commanded by its chieftain as colonel, as long as he was of sufficient age. Younger brothers held next descending ranks or senior cadet branches of the family provided respectively the lieutenant colonel, the major and so on. Each company in the regiment was formed from a cadet branch of the clan or the men of a particular district and was led by two captains, two lieutenants and ensigns.

The first rank of the formation was made up of the daoine uaisle, *the 'gentlemen of the clan', all of whom were by tradition provided with targes and were therefore better armed than the rear ranks. On the day of battle, each company provided two of their best men to be a bodyguard for the chief and consanguinity or close blood-relationship would always be considered in making such choice. The chief positioned himself in the centre of the column by the colours where he stood between two brothers, two cousins-german – the* mac-brathair-athar *of Gaelic tradition – or other close relations. The rank and file of the clan, the* sluagh, *always arranged themselves with close regard for their relationship, with father, son and brother standing next to each other. Thus the social leadership of the clan hierarchy as well as kinship, real or imagined, with the leaders supplied a strongly cohesive force.*

Highland society was drawn into the wider forum of Scottish politics and also into national politics with profound effects. From 1639, the clans were recruited into the cause of the Covenants, Royalist risings and subsequent support for the Stuart kings, before and after their forfeiture of the Scottish Crown in 1689. More warriors were required to fill the ranks. The adherence or antagonism of some clans and families to the Crown established deep divisions which had become hardened by the eighteenth century. This could be said to have dissipated the cultural and military potential of Gaelic society glimpsed briefly from time to time in the medieval and early modern periods and invigorated by the notion of a pan-Celtic alliance of Scotland and Ireland against the 'Saxon' in the face of the Tudor reconquest of the sixteenth century.

Even though many of their leaders opposed the Jacobites and supported the government in the campaign of 1745-6, and many of the country folk were reluctant to leave their homes when pressed to join the clan regiments, there remained a strong strain of loyalty to the Stuarts. The famous Gaelic poet, Duncan Ban Macintyre, did not just speak for himself in expressing a preference for Prince Charles though he himself was then serving in the government's Argyll Militia:

'Terrible is our plight the young Prince
Should be in great adversity,
And that where he ought to be established
King George is in occupation.
Knowledgeable folk are telling us
That he had no claim on London ...'

In this period of persistent warfare, it was important for individuals and families to belong to a strong organisation. Clans grew and coalesced round strong leaders and successful families, and equally, when the family of the chief was exterminated, the clan would break up. The MacLeods of Lewis, the MacIains of Ardnamurchan, and the MacDonalds of Lochalsh and Islay are examples of this process of reduction. The chiefs were dependent on a powerful following for the holding of lands and often absorbed lesser kindreds settled within

their territories. In Lochaber for example, the MacMartins, the MacSorlies and the MacGillonies were forced by various means to take the name of Cameron.

Gaelic society was coming under siege in the seventeenth century but also asserting itself and resisting the attacks when they came. While the predominance of the Lordship of the Isles was destroyed, most obviously by forfeiture to the Crown, the other branches of Clan Donald carried the torch of political and cultural leadership and tried to counter a shift of power to leading families such as the Campbells of Argyll and the Mackenzies. The latter were operating as agents of the government with delegated administrative and judicial powers. This situation in which the Crown would set clan against clan could create intense enmity, between MacDonalds and Campbells for example, which was sharpened to bitter conflict and undying hatred by events such as the Battle of Inverlochy in 1645 and the Massacre of Glencoe in 1692.

It is a further paradox of Scottish history and culture that in many respects Gaelic culture appeared to thrive in the seventeenth century. Poetry and music evolved and changed, taking forward ancient traditions and characteristics and borrowing and developing new ones. A learned and formal literary language shared with medieval Ireland began to wither and a vernacular Scottish Gaelic emerges into history mainly in the form of song. The structure and rhythm of the newer song-poetry is comparable to bagpipe music which also appears to have flourished in the Highlands and Islands in this period.

The bagpipe, with a wide distribution in Europe and Asia and evolving as the universal musical instrument in medieval Europe, was adopted in the Highlands at a comparatively late date and probably in the sixteenth century. It is not mentioned in any of the old Gaelic tales or in surviving medieval Gaelic verse: the clarsach or harp was the chosen instrument of the aristocracy and literati and used together with Gaelic song, distinctive melodies, rhythms and styles which were adopted into bagpipe music.

In the same way as the bards and harpers of medieval Gaelic society passed on their craft and skills to successive generations of the same families, the pipers too came to be grafted on to Gaelic society. It was widely accepted that the masters of the art of piping, of piobaireachd*, were the MacCrimmons, the hereditary pipers to the MacLeods of Dunvegan. The households of the great chiefs such as MacLeod of Dunvegan were traditionally full of poets and musicians. The standards and tastes set in the great halls were emulated and maintained in the houses of tacksmen. The MacLeods of Talisker, for example, entertained poets, reciters, singers, harpers, fiddlers and pipers, all of whom enjoyed the hospitality of the laird and exchanged their respective arts.*

The bagpipe developed a distinctive and strident form in Gaelic society, the piob mhor *or great Highland bagpipe, which barely survived the period of proscription following the '45. But with its highly developed technique and sophisticated musical forms inherited from Gaelic society, it was not likely to succumb easily. Mackintosh of Mackintosh described the piping tradition in the Highlands in the mid-eighteenth century:*

'The piper was a man of such Consequence, that he had a Boy attending to carry his pipe when he did not play. The pipe was decorated with Ribbands of the same colour with the livery of the family; his duty was in peace to play morning and evening in front of the

Castle, and in War to call the Clan to Arms, to inspire them in the fight, and give them notice to retreat when necessary, which three parts of Duty are well expressed in the pipe Marches. Frequently in the harvest, the Reapers cut the Corn regularly to a tune, which Custom is still preserved in the Isle of Skye, where the only good pipers are reared and to be found, for there, regular Colledges are formed for instructing youth in using that Martial Instrument.'

Though the battle-lines became vividly and unequivocally drawn between Lowlands and Highlands, the Gaels continued to support the Stuarts throughout the seventeenth and eighteenth centuries because of their fundamental loyalty to the line of native kings whose ancestry stretched back to the historical kings of Dal Riada in the fifth century. Their descent in turn from a prehistoric and even mythical race of kings was well known in Gaelic tradition with its strong sense of history. It was lovingly extolled by the bards and served to exemplify the spiritual and cultural unity of a Celtic people and lingua franca stretching from the Butt of Lewis to Cape Clear.

Support for Jacobitism drew some of its inspiration from this spiritual and cultural unity and from a belief in the potential of a pan-Gaelic or Celtic movement and the concept that the whole of Scotland was once wholly Gaelic. A belief that the Gaels would regain their rightful place was formulated by Highland prophets such as the 'Brahan Seer' and this almost messianic theme was psychologically significant in Highland support for the Jacobites.

As we have seen, Highland and Gaelic culture was a strong and distinctive force within Scotland, and one which came to be used, if not exploited, by Jacobitism and the exiled Stuarts. In the rapidly changing currents of early eighteenth-century politics, when Jacobitism was a pawn of French imperialism, Prince Charles Edward Stuart was persuaded to launch his campaign to regain the throne for his father in the Highlands. He was appealing for support in the most conservative areas of Scottish society or those areas which had seen less of the benefits of Union as might persuade them to forego their traditional support for the Stuarts or forget their distrust and dislike of the Lowland Scots and English. Landing in the old Roman Catholic enclave of Moidart, in the mainland territories of MacDonald of Clanranald, the Prince met among others Alexander MacDonald, the greatest of all Gaelic poets, whom he questioned about Highland dress. The poet described how '... in such times of danger or during a war, we had a different method of using the plaid, that with one spring I could start to my feet with drawn sword and cocked pistol in my hand ...' The poet was also a powerful propagandist for the Jacobite cause as well as holding a commission in the Prince's army. His 'Song for the Prince' which is still sung was a pre-campaign song designed to arouse enthusiasm:

'O hi ri ri, tha e tighinn,
O hi ri ri, 'n Righ tha bhuainn ...'

'He is coming, our exiled King
Let us take our arms and our garb
And the flowing tartan plaid.'

Following the Rising and the consequent legislation against Highland dress and tartan,

the poet praised the tartan as the symbol of his race and of the warrior Gael. The long and vigorous song opens with

'B' fhearr leam breacan uallach ...'

'Better is the proud tartan plaid
Around my shoulder and under my arm,
Better than though I would get a coat
Of the best cloth that comes from England.'

Prince Charles was presented with a gift of Highland dress by Scottish Jacobites before 1745. He understood the symbolic value of tartan and ensured that it was adopted as the uniform of his army. Tartan had become a symbol of Jacobitism and the Prince's army a 'tartan army'. For better or worse, tartan survived to be adopted as a form of national dress for all Scots, providing a powerful form of identity and symbolic reference to the ancient culture of the Gael which has done so much to shape Scotland.

Introduction

BLAIR CASTLE,
BLAIR ATHOLL, PERTHSHIRE,
PH18 5TJ

14th July, 1995

I feel very honoured to be asked to write an introduction to the Catalogue prepared by The National Trust for Scotland, of which I am President, to accompany the exhibition *The Swords and the Sorrows* at Culloden. This exhibition, opening on the 250th anniversary of the fateful Battle of Culloden, brings together from collections all over Britain items that have not returned to Culloden since that day, and marks The National Trust for Scotland's commemoration of the '45 and Culloden in a very special way.

The title chosen for this exhibition shows an awareness of what the '45 meant to Scotland – swords, and sorrows (in plenty) to families on both sides of what was a civil war. My own family had divided loyalties, with the 2nd Duke remaining staunchly Hanoverian, going off to Bath for the cure and remaining there during the course of the Rising; and Lord George Murray, his younger brother, becoming the military genius of the Jacobite army, fighting for a cause he deeply believed in at a time when he could have remained quietly at home improving his estates. But the Stuart cause could make men give up everything they held dear – at a distance of 250 years, hindsight makes us think that they were foolish to do so, but matters were not so clear-cut in 1745. The still unpopular Union of 1707 rankled with many Scots who felt that they had lost control over their own affairs, and the Jacobite Risings were partly an attempt to effect a cure for this. To the men of the time, as demonstrated in their letters and diaries, the Risings were civil wars, and the Stuart cause was not lost until Derby – if even then – for the Stuarts could inspire great loyalty.

My family played their part in the Rising of 1745, and a distinguished part at that: their record of loyalty, and their honourable conduct throughout the course of the '45, remains an inspiration to later generations of Scots. This exhibition tells both sides of the story, and the catalogue will be available to both sides of the contest – I hope that my introduction will do a little to counter that of the Duke of Argyll. However, since the '45 our families have become good friends, as have our clans, and there is now little between us. In 1745 it was perhaps the clan that made us take such diametrically opposite sides, rather than any personal animosity.

Atholl.

Inveraray Castle
Argyll
Scotland
PA32 8XF

I am delighted this exhibition debunks the all too common misconception that the 1745 Rebellion was an affair of Scots versus English.

On the contrary, more Scots, my own clan and family among them, took arms against the Young Pretender than for him. Even in the Highlands, where the Northern clans were staunchly Hanoverian, the Jacobite support came largely from those whose motivations were at least as much to get their own back on the Campbells as they were to restore the Stewarts to the British throne. Thus at Culloden, the Jacobite army included French, Irish and English.

But the romanticism of 19th century Edinburgh drawing rooms has for too long overlaid the whole episode with a gaudily coloured haze of romanticism. Like the Devil, one has to admit that the Jacobites have all the best tunes. But this distorting of history does nobody any good and the truth, as is shown here, was far different.

In reality, like all civil wars, the 1745 Rebellion was a tragedy with neighbour pitched against neighbour, brother against brother. The vast majority of the Clan Campbell fought staunchly for the Hanoverian succession and the Protestant faith to which my ancestors long adhered, the Marquis of Argyll and his son, the 9th Earl, both going to the scaffold for their religious beliefs.

I feel deeply sorry for that tragic figure Prince Charles Edward but am profoundly thankful that he never got to the British throne and am extremely proud that my forebears and our clan played a part in preventing such a disaster.

But it is possible to salute the courage of brave men - on both sides - while fervently hoping that Culloden was indeed the end of an old song whose tune, pray God, will never be played again.

Argyll

Scottish swords and the '45

By A V B Norman

The importance of the sword to the medieval inhabitants of the Western Highlands of Scotland is shown by the frequency with which it is represented on carved tombstones of the area, either alone or girded to the side of a sepulchral effigy. These swords appear to be single-handed weapons with straight blades, and were probably mainly two-edged. The hilts with their lobated pommels indicate their Viking ancestry. The straight quillons are usually slightly inclined towards the blade and are sometimes spatulate-ended. The earliest extant swords of this type are thought to date from the early 15th century because of their resemblance to the sword engraved on the tombstone in Kinkell kirkyard of Gilbert de Greenlaw, who fell at Harlaw in 1411.

Swords with somewhat similar hilts but of greater size begin to be represented on Highland tombstones early in the 16th century; there is one dated 1539 at Oronsay Priory, the quillons each end in pierced quatrefoil. In surviving swords of this type a pair of stout langets flanks the blade arising at the junction of the quillons. This is the two-handed weapon until recently called by collectors a claymore (from the Gaelic claidheamh mòr, *the great sword), a term which should be used only for the basket-hilted broadsword.*[1] *The correct term is now known to be* claidheamh dà làimh.[2]

It is not at all clear when the basket-hilted sword was introduced to the Highlands: apparently no representation occurs on the carved stones of the area. However, the use of the phrase 'Irish hilt' for a basket hilt was fairly widespread in English documents from about 1620, 'Irish' in this case meaning Gaelic. This presumably indicates that by this time the basket hilt was regarded as characteristic of the Scottish Highlands.

1 C Blair, 'The word claymore', in Caldwell, pp 378-2, with a postscript by S Maxwell, pp 383-4.

2 I am very grateful to Mr Blair for drawing my attention to this reference which had been passed to him by Donald Wilson.

Illustration of Clansman by Jenny Proudfoot

THE EXHIBITS

1:1 Two-handed Highland sword (claidheamh dà làimh)

Hilt, Scottish Highland, late medieval; blade German (Solingen or Passau), probably early 16th century.

The iron hilt consists of a small wheel-pommel, with the 'hub' off-centre towards the blade, and a longitudinally-faceted quillon-block supporting a pair of long quillons of flattened-hexagonal section inclined towards the blade, between which is a pair of square-ended langets flanking the blade. Each quillon ends in an openwork quatrefoil formed of four short tubes welded together.

The grip is covered with dark brown leather.

The straight two-edged blade is of lenticular section, and has a shallow central hollow for approximately 11" from the hilt on each face. Incised on one face with a short-coupled and very stylised wolf, and on the other with an orb, the arms of its cross triple-forked. There are traces of brass in each mark.

Length overall, 54 $^{1}/_{16}$".

Swords similar to 1:1 are frequently carved on late medieval and early 16h-century gravestones in the Western Highlands and Islands.[1] However, some surviving examples belong to families such as the Forbeses in the Eastern Highlands. The survival in both Highland and Lowland Scotland of so many two-handed swords is probably connected with their use as bearing swords in the courts of baronies, which survived until the abolition of heritable jurisdiction in 1747.

The wolf was originally the town mark of Passau in Bavaria, but was subsequently taken over by Solingen in North Rhineland-Westphalia, the major German centre for the manufacture and export of blades.[2] Blades were made there to suit various markets, including broad blades for Scotland.

Lender: The National Trust for Scotland (Fyvie Castle).

1 Steer & Bannerman.

2 Schmid, pp 317-42.

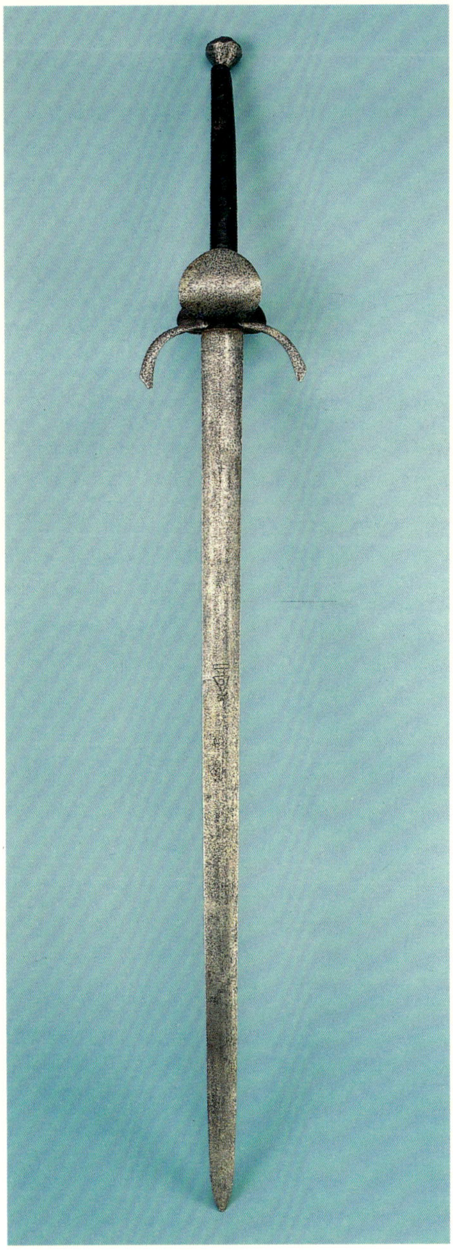

1:2 Two-handed Highland sword (claidheamh dà làimh)

Hilt, probably Scottish, late 16th- or early 17th-century; blade, German (Solingen or Passau) late medieval.

The iron hilt consists of a pommel, the part away from the blade deeply cut with grooves radiating from the apex, and a pair of long quillons, of flattened lenticular section, deeply arched towards the blade, supporting at their centre on each face an oval shell curved towards the pommel and concave towards the hand. Both quillons are slightly inclined outward. The end of each is crudely shaped as the head of a serpent(?). The leather lining of the shells is now missing.

The grip is covered with dark-brown leather tooled at intervals with small quatrefoils of oak leaves.

The straight, two-edged blade was originally of flattened-hexagonal section, but is now worn to a lenticular section. Incised on each face with three devices, originally inlaid with brass; 1) upon a recumbent S a cross; 2) the remains of a short-coupled wolf; and 3) a device shaped like a bishop's mitre upon a waisted stand, with at the apex of the mitre a cross, the ends of its arms triple-forked. On the front of the 'mitre' is a cinquefoil.

Length overall, 57$^{3}/_{16}$".

The phrase 'ane pair of clam schellit gairdis', found in the records of the Edinburgh Hammermen in January 1583/4, probably refers to a hilt like this.[1] The blade is probably from an earlier sword, which was re-hilted to bring it back into fashion, exactly what happened to the so-called Sword of Wallace, which was given a new hilt and pommel by Robert Selkyrk, the Royal Cutler, in December 1505.[2]

This was probably the bearing sword for the Court of Barony.

Lender: Tam Dalyell (The House of the Binns).

1 C Blair, 'The early basket-hilt in Britain', in Caldwell, p 159 & n 29.

2 Accounts of the Lord High Treasurers of Scotland, III, Edinburgh 1901, p 175.

1:3 *Two-handed Highland sword* (claidheamh dà làimh)

Hilt, Scottish, late 16th- or early 17th-century; blade, possibly German, probably contemporary with the hilt.

The iron hilt consists of a pommel with a very prominent tang-button, and guards similar to those of 1:2, except that the quillons are shorter and less curved (possibly trimmed back). The shells contain fragments of the leather lining. The quillons now have a span of only $7^{31}/_{32}$", having been severely cropped at some time.

The grip is covered with brown leather and bound at intervals with a twist of copper wire. There is a fringe of dull red wool between the grip and the pommel.

The straight, two-edged blade, is of flattened lenticular section, with a narrow central fuller, all very worn.

Length overall, 51".

The catalogue of the Armoury of George IV records that this sword was received in March 1822 from the collection of George III (No 3151). It is probably 'A two handed broad sword' in the post-mortem inventory of William Augustus, Duke of Cumberland (1721-65), whose collection passed to George III.[1] Presumably the Duke had acquired it during the campaign of 1746.

The 'twig mark' on the inner face of the blade, which resembles the Greek letter π under a crudely drawn crown, is thought to be a North Italian bladesmith's mark,[2] but it was widely copied.

Not exhibited. Photograph: The Royal Collection © Her Majesty The Queen.

1 Royal Archives, Cumberland Papers, Vol I, p 63.

2 See, for example, a sabre in the Old Imperial Armoury at Vienna, Inv No A123 (Boccia & Coelho, p 340, No 134).

Literature: Laking, *European Armour*, fig 690.

William Augustus, Duke of Cumberland, by a painter of the circle of Van Loo (c1739)

1:4 *Two-handed sword*

Hilt, probably Lowland Scottish[1], possibly about 1525-50; blade, German (Solingen or Passau).

The iron hilt consists of a pommel with a very prominent tang-button, and a pair of quillons of circular section supporting a large side-ring at their centre on each face. At the centre of the quillons is a pair of langets flanking the blade. The quillons taper evenly towards the terminal knobs, which are turned sharply towards the blade. Each side-ring is bridged by a cruciform guard with a quatrefoil plate at its centre.

The grip is covered with modern leather.

The straight, two-edged blade, which is of lenticular section, has a ricasso $6^{3}/_{4}$" long, and a central fuller on each face. Deeply struck on each face near the hilt with a hexagonal punch framing, what appears to be either a stylised hand (possibly the mark of Antwerp) or a crown with five rays. A very similar mark occurs on a sword in the Museum of Antiquities, Edinburgh (reg no LA6). Incised just beyond the end of the fuller on one side with a stylised wolf, and on the other with the remains of an orb.

Length overall, $68^{3}/_{4}$".

Lender: The National Trust for Scotland (House of Dun).

1 See Wallace, pp 11-12, & figs 9-11, who dates the type to the late 16th century.

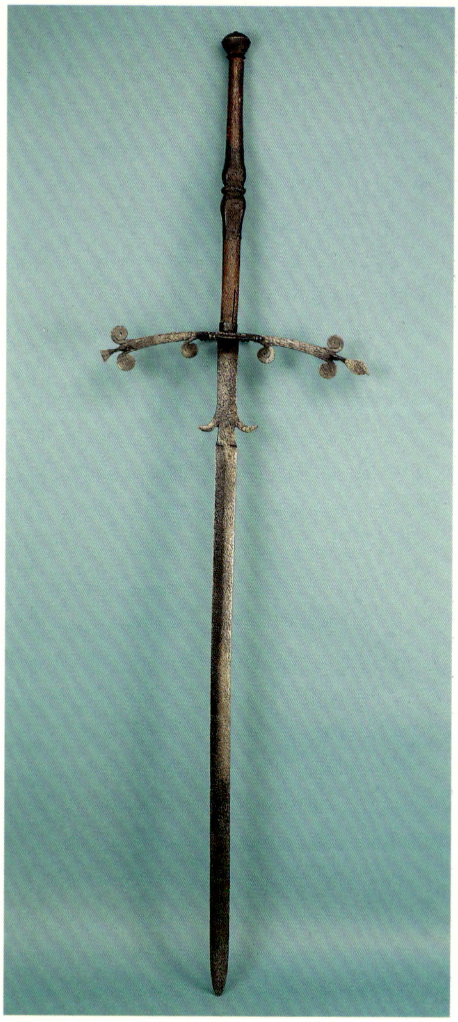

1:5 *Two-handed sword*

Probably Swiss or South German, late 16th-century.

The iron hilt consists of a modern pommel, and a pair of long quillons of rectangular section supporting a large side-ring at their centre on each face, and a pair of vestigial arms of the hilt tightly scrolled towards the blade. Each quillon ends in a fleur-de-lis-like terminal. The terminal petal at one end is engraved with a fish's head, that at the other represents its tail. Both faces of the quillons are deeply engraved with candelabra-like foliage. The side-rings are of diamond-section and are each fitted with two collars. The plate mounted on the centre of the quillons on each side is engraved with a spray of stylised foliage.

The baluster-shaped grip now lacks its cover.

The straight, two-edged blade, which is of flattened-diamond section, has a ricasso $8^{1}/_{8}$" long, projecting from each edge of which is an acute lug curving gently forward. The forward end of the ricasso is struck on one face with a shield-shaped punch framing two separate deer's antlers inverted.

Length overall, $73^{1}/_{4}$".

Comparable swords are to be found in several Swiss arsenals.[1] Originally the ricasso would have been covered with leather, to allow it to be gripped by the left hand when using the sword at close quarters.

Lender: The National Trust for Scotland (Crathes Castle).

1 For a very similar example from Zurich, see Schneider, No 152.

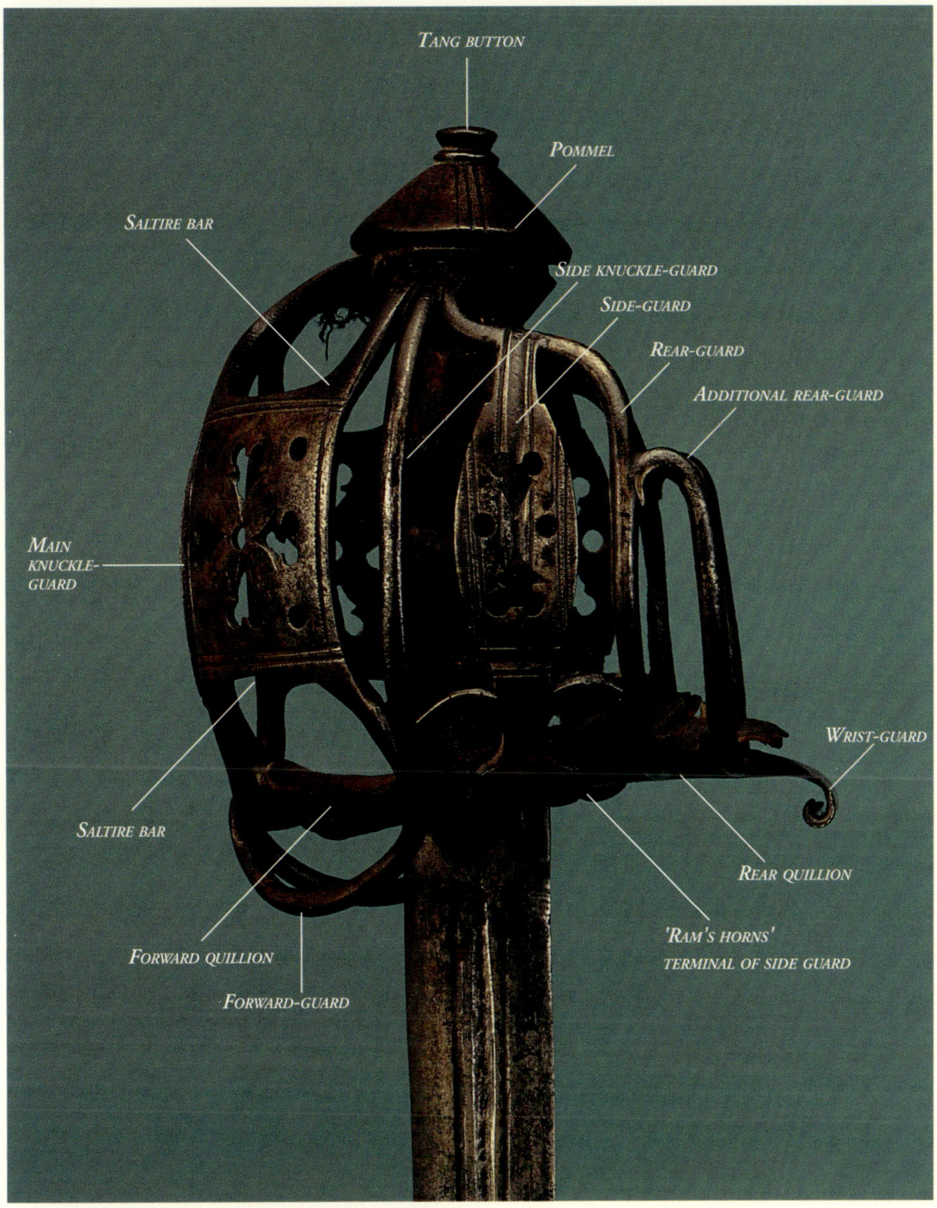

BASKET-HILTED SWORDS [1]

The classic form of basket-hilt was developed from a mid-16th-century precursor which enclosed the hand in a cage of nine narrow bars arising on the long recurved quillons and curving round to join up in three groups just before they touched the rather large globular pommel. Except for a few early examples in which the guards outside the hand differ in formation from those inside, in all surviving hilts the two bars adjacent to the main knuckle-guard on each side are crossed in saltire.

From about 1560, apparently, the basket hilt was being made frontally symmetrical; that is, the inside was a mirror image of the outside. The area in front of the forefinger, where it was crossed over the quillon, was protected by a pair of forward-guards growing out of the forward quillon. These diverge and each curves round, one on the outside and one on the inside, to join the bar forming the side knuckle-guard near its root, and then continues back to join the rear-guard in the same way.

This simple form survived well into the 17th century but, by that date, the forward quillon no longer projected beyond the perimeter of the basket, and the rear one usually projected only slightly, if at all. In order to give additional protection to the area of the wrist, the rearward extension of the forward-guards between the side knuckle-guard and the rear-guard was given a lug projecting towards the quillon. By the end of the 17th century this relatively simple form of guard had become the fully-fledged basket hilt with most of the features still found on the claymore of the Scottish regiments today. The earliest illustration of such a hilt is in the portrait at Inveraray of the 1st Duke of Argyll by Medina, painted about 1690. The precise sequence of this development and the rate at which it took place is still unclear, but the most obvious improvement was the addition of further guards to the rear of the hilt.

To give greater protection to the wrist, the hilt was extended by the addition of a subsidiary rear-guard. This arose on an extension of the rear quillon and lay parallel to the main rear-guard, curving round to join it usually at about half its length. The additional rear-guard on the outer side was often longer than that on the inner side. The continuation to the rear of the forward-guards, which linked the side knuckle-guard and the rear-guard, was replaced by a separate bar, at first T-shaped and subsequently cruciform. The ends of the arms of this cross sometimes curved towards the blade.

Eventually the end of the cross towards the pommel was prolonged to become a fairly wide side-guard joining the rear-guard near its end as it curves over to join the end of the side knuckle-guard. What had been the ends of the arms of the original cross were now usually curved towards the blade like a ram's horns. By this phase of the development the swellings at the intersections of the saltires had become hexagonal. They later grew much larger and became rectangular with the arms of the saltire supporting them at their corners.

By the end of the century, there was a tendency for the rear-guards, which had formerly sloped slightly towards the pommel, to lie parallel to the side knuckle-guards for most of their length. Whatever form the decoration took, the broader longitudinal guards were very often decorated with parallel engraved lines and flutes.

The rectangular plates at the centres of the saltires were described by Walter Allan, the Stirling swordsmith, in a letter of 11 December 1745, as 'the two broad sheelds'.[2] *They and the broad central areas of the side-guards and of the main knuckle-guard were often decorated with engraved lines and sometimes with circles, and usually pierced with small holes of various shapes, described by Allan in the same letter as 'harts' and 'clibs'. The edges of all these plates were usually cut with cusps, angular projections, and merlons; any straight edges left between the projections being bevelled with the file. A narrow flute usually follows each edge of the shields.*

At some time, perhaps as early as 1700, a T-shaped wrist-guard, often of considerable width, began to be forged on to the end of the rear quillon, its cross-bar tightly scrolled towards the blade. Many older hilts seem to have been brought up to date at this time by having a wrist-guard riveted on.

1 For the history of the early basket hilt, see C Blair, 'The early basket-hilt in Britain', in Caldwell, pp 151-252; for the history of the later types, see Wallace.

2 S Maxwell, 'Letters from Walter Allan, Armourer in Stirling, to Colin Mitchell, Goldsmith in Canongate, 1741-1751,' in Caldwell, pp 408-418.

Illustration of Clansman by Jenny Proudfoot

1:6 *Basket-hilted sabre* (claidheam-crom)

Hilt, Scottish, probably about 1690; blade, German (probably Solingen) dated 1662.

The iron hilt consists of a large pommel with a step for the ends of the guards, and a basket of fully-developed Highland type (including the additional rear-guards, but no wrist-guard) with stout bars of rectangular section, longitudinally fluted. The edges of the main knuckle-guard, the side-guards, and the broad shields are all cusped and crenellated. The piercing on the broad guards includes 'hearts' made up of three holes conjoined, two round and one rectangular.

The grip is covered with the skin of a black dogfish and is bound with a twist of gilt copper wire. The full liner of buff-leather is later.

The curved, one-edged blade has two broad, full-length fullers. The spine of the blade has been ground down about $^1/_8$", starting $12^1/_2$" from the hilt. It is etched in line with gilding in the lines, with Latin mottoes, military trophies, warriors on prancing horses, classical heads, a lion rampant, and *Anno Domini 1662.*

The black leather scabbard has three iron mounts, a mouthpiece, a belt-hook and a crampet. It may be a replacement in the working life of the sword.

Length overall, $37^3/_4$".

The basket of 1:6 is typologically early in that it is steeply canted in relationship to the main axis of the sword, has a very small opening for the hand, and has no wrist-guard. A closely comparable hilt is illustrated in Medina's portrait of Archibald Campbell, 1st Duke of Argyll, painted about 1690, at Inveraray (cat 10:21).

A basket-hilted sabre is illustrated in Richard Waitt's portrait of Alistair Grant, the Champion of Clan Grant, painted in 1714.[1] In 1695 the assay of Archibald Simpson I, armourer in Glasgow, was 'ane mounted shable [sabre] with ane hieland hilt'. The sword of Charles Stewart of Ardsheil is described as 'a claymore called the Turk (*Turcael*)'. The name may have come from the blade being curved in Turkish style.[2]

Lender: The Duke of Buccleuch (Boughton House).

Possibly acquired from the family of the Dukes of Argyll by marriage. Caroline, daughter and heiress of John, 2nd Duke of Argyll, was the mother of Henry, 3rd Duke of Buccleuch.

1 Dunbar, frontispiece.

2 Whitelaw, *Scottish Arms Makers*, p 221. MacKenzie, Vol I, p 179.

Literature: Norman, in *Boughton House*, pp 225 & Pl 97.

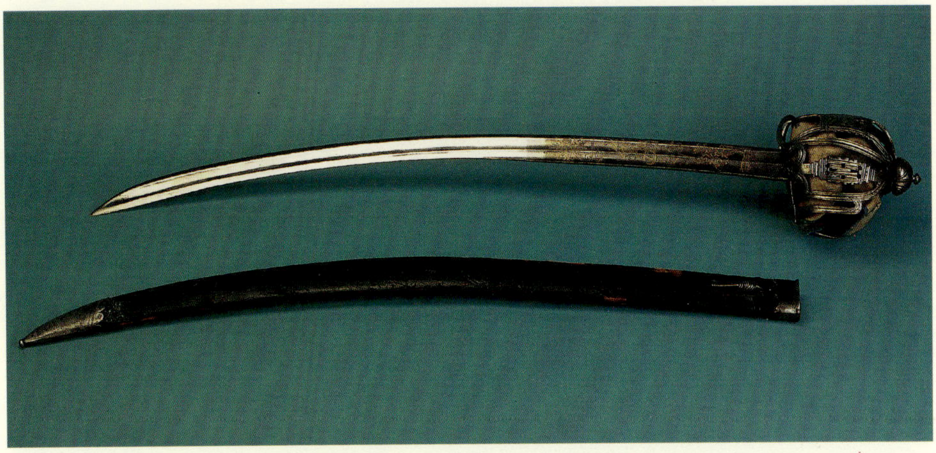

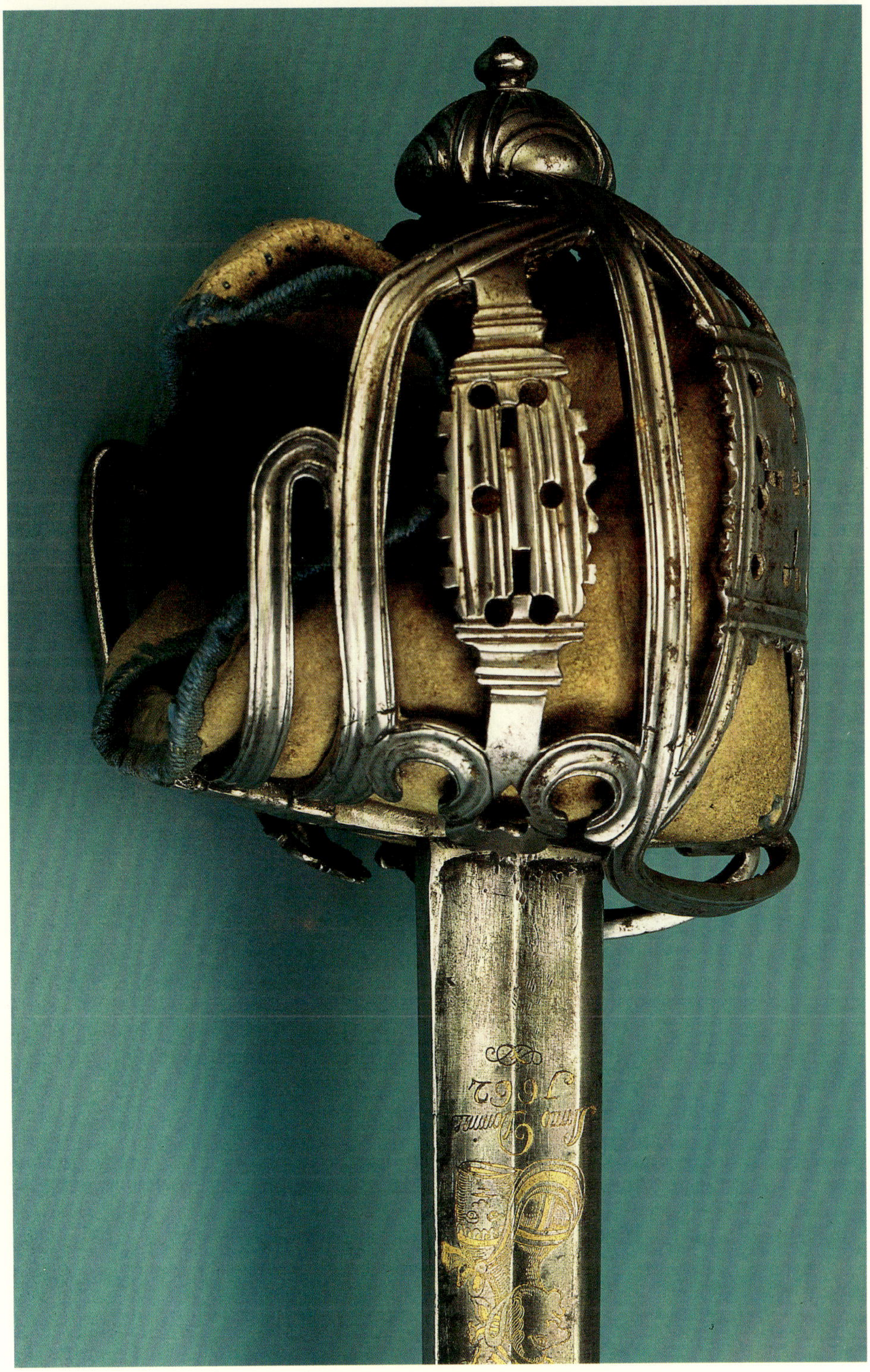

Archibald Campbell, 1st Duke of Argyll, by Medina.

1:7 Basket-hilted horseman's backsword (claidheamh cùil)

Hilt, Scottish (Glasgow), early 18th-century; blade, German or British, probably of the middle years of the century.

The iron hilt is similar to that of 1:6, except that the inner shield is replaced by a large oval ring, and there is a small scrolled wrist-guard. Stamped on the rear quillon towards the hand are the letters I S over G.

The grip is covered with black rayskin and bound at close intervals with twists of brass wire. The three-quarter liner is of buff leather.

The straight, one-edged blade has two contiguous fullers, a narrow one at the spine and a broad, full-length one, and a false edge $15^{5}/_{8}$" long.

Length overall, $37^{1}/_{4}$".

The initials on the quillon are thought to be those of one of the two John Simpsons, father and son, armourers in Glasgow.[1] The older man was admitted to the Incorporation of Hammermen in 1683, was appointed King's Armourer in 1715, and was dead by 1717. The younger man was admitted to the Incorporation in 1711, and was dead by 1749.[2] Probably they both used the same mark, but the younger differentiated his mark by placing a small Y after the S, presumably standing for 'Younger'.[3]

The oval ring on the inner side of the basket is thought to have been either to allow the sword to be held in the left hand by the basket, thus freeing the right hand for the pistol, or to allow the reins to be shortened without withdrawing the right hand from the hilt. The blade is of a type popular for British cavalry, *c*1720-70.

Lender: Geoffrey Jenkinson.

1 Whitelaw, in *Transactions*, pp 19-20.

2 Whitelaw, *Scottish Arms Makers*, p 221.

3 Norman, in *Despatch*.

1:8 Basket-hilted broadsword (claidheamh mòr)

Hilt, Scottish (Glasgow), early 18th-century; blade, German (probably Solingen), probably contemporary with the hilt.The iron hilt is similar to that of 1:6, except that the pommel is biconical and there is a small triangular scrolled wrist-guard. The edges of all the broader guards are invected. The piercing includes a star of six at the centre of each shield. Stamped on the rear quillon towards the hand are the letters IS over G.

The grip is modern.

The straight, two-edged blade has a narrow fuller close to each edge, $30^{7}/_{8}$" long, starting at the hilt, and two more narrow fullers, 24" long, starting $6^{3}/_{4}$" from the hilt. Struck five times on each face is the mark of a Turk's head viewed from his left. The point is broken off.

Length overall, $37^{5}/_{16}$".

The hilt-maker's initials are discussed under 1:7. The bladesmith's mark has not been recorded at Solingen, but is similar in character to several of those which have.

Lender: Geoffrey Jenkinson.

1:9 Basket-hilted broadsword (claidheamh mòr)

Hilt, Scottish, second quarter 18th century; blade, German (Solingen), possibly contemporary with the hilt or earlier.

The iron hilt is similar to that of 1:6, except that the bars are more slender and the workmanship less exact. Each edge of the shields has a broad merlon at its centre. The edges of the broad guards are cut with small inlets with lobated ends. The piercing includes 'hearts' made up of three separate holes, a rectangular one slightly bevelled to fit between two round ones. The end of the rear quillon projects slightly beyond the basket and is struck on the side towards the blade with a letter, either M or W.

The grip is missing. Inside the basket are the remains of the thick piece of buff leather that prevented a point from entering the guards, and of the woollen fringe that prevented the underside of the pommel from chafing the hand.

The straight, two-edged blade, which is of flattened-hexagonal section for 6" near the hilt, becoming lenticular thereafter, has a ricasso $2^{9}/_{32}$" long. Stamped on the outer face is AN DR EA, and on the inner face FA RA RA. Struck before and after each word and between each pair of letters is the mark of a king's head viewed from his left. Struck on each face of the ricasso is a small shield of arms: quarterly, 1 & 4, France, 2, Scotland, and 3, Ireland.

Length overall, $39^{5}/_{16}$".

The signature on the blade purports to be that of Andrea dei Ferari, a swordsmith working in Belluno, a small town in the mountains north of Venice. First recorded in 1567, he was already described as a 'talented master'. His name occurs on German blades intended for the Scottish market until the early 19th century. But very few of the blades bearing his name are early enough to be his work.[1] The bladesmith's mark is one of many variants used by members of the Wundes family of Solingen.[2] The significance of the armorial mark, which occurs with variations of its quarterings, is unknown (see also 1:38).

Lender: Geoffrey Jenkinson.

1 *Wallace Collection Catalogues*, pp 127-8, *sub* No 544.

2 Weyersberg, pp 57-61.

1:10 Basket-hilted backsword (claidheamh cùil)

Hilt, Scottish, second quarter 18th century; blade, German (Solingen), probably contemporary with the hilt.

The iron hilt is similar to that of 1:6, except that the bars are more slender, the workmanship less exact, and the conventional fluting of the broad guards lacking. (The wrist-guard has been broken off.) The edges of the broad guards are cut with long scallops alternating with pairs of fishtail merlons flanking small U-shaped inlets. The piercing includes 'hearts' of conventional shape.

The grip is of marbled bone.

The straight, one-edged blade has a ricasso 2 1/2" long, two narrow contiguous fullers and a false edge 10" long. Stamped on each face in the fullers is

SS ANDRIA *SS*
SS FARARA *SS*.

Struck on each face of the ricasso with an almost illegible mark of a king's head viewed from his left.

Length overall, 39 11/16".

For the king's head mark, see under 1:9.

Lender: Geoffrey Jenkinson.

1:11 Basket-hilted horseman's backsword (claidheamh cùil)

Hilt, Scottish (Glasgow), possibly between 1709 and 1717; blade, probably German, possibly late 17th-century.

The iron hilt is similar to that of 1:7 (the wrist-guard has been broken off). The edges of all the broad guards are cut with pairs of fishtail merlons flanking either obtuse points or U-shaped inlets. The piercing includes 'hearts' made up of three separate holes, a diamond one shaped to fit between the other two which are round. Stamped on the rear quillon towards the hand are the letters TG over G.

The grip, liner, and silk fringe are all modern.

The straight, one-edged blade has a ricasso 1 3/8" long, two narrow contiguous fullers, and a false edge 7" long. Etched in black line on each face with stylised flowering plants and the words *Andrea/farara* written transversely.

Length overall, 40 1/16".

The initials on the quillon are thought to be those of Thomas Gemmill, armourer in Glasgow.[1] He was appointed King's Armourer on 18 January 1718. Presumably he was the same man as Thomas Gammill, hammerman, admitted burgess of Glasgow in 1709.[2] Since several hilts are known signed with his name and title, 1:11, signed only with his initials, may date before his royal appointment.

Lender: Geoffrey Jenkinson.

1 Whitelaw, in *Transactions*, pp 22-3.

2. Whitelaw, *Scottish Arms Makers*, pp 217 & 224.

1:12 Basket-hilted horseman's backsword (claidheamh cùil)

Hilt, Scottish, second quarter 18th century; blade, German (Solingen), probably late 17th-century.

The iron hilt is similar to that of 1:6, except that the pommel is biconical, the bars are not fluted, and the workmanship is less exact (the wrist-guard has been broken off). The edges of the broad guards are cut like those of 1:7. The piercing includes 'hearts' like those of 1:17. Struck on the rear quillon towards the blade is a letter A with a truncated apex.

The grip is covered with the black skin of a dogfish. There is a later piece of leather inside the basket, and a woollen fringe of red, yellow and green.

The straight, one-edged blade is similar to that of 1:11. The ricasso is worn away. There are traces of line etching near the hilt.

Length overall, 39 9/16".

Lender: Geoffrey Jenkinson.

1:13 Basket-hilted broadsword (claidheamh mòr)

Hilt, Scottish (Stirling), probably first quarter 18th century; blade, probably German, of 17th-century type.

The iron hilt consists of a pommel and a basket of fully-developed Highland type, with long additional rear-guards and a broad scrolled wrist-guard. The bars are of circular section. The ends of each of the longitudinal bars are flanked on each side by two pairs of claws. The edges of the broad guards are all cut with small fishtail merlons alternating either with scallops or obtuse points. The conventional fluting of the broad guards is lacking. There is no piercing, its place being taken by 'hearts', quatrefoils, and twists all inlaid in gold. Stuck on the rear quillon towards the blade are the letters J A over S.

The grip is carved with three rows of interlace like the haft of a dirk. Brass ferrules.

The straight two-edged blade has a ricasso $2^1/_8$" long, and three narrow, contiguous fullers. Stamped in the fullers on each face is X)I(X XIIX X)I(X: ANDRIA X FARARA: X)I(X XIIX X)I(X.

Length overall, $41^3/_4$".

The marks on the hilt have been identified as those of one of the two John Allans, both armourers in Stirling.[1] The elder man was admitted burgess of Stirling in 1714, and his son in 1741.[2] Charles Whitelaw's theory that the father signed with roman letters and the son with italic letters, was disproved by C Rolland in 1990.[3] The type of flat inlay with precious metal found on the hilt may indicate the influence of the pistol-makers of Doune, where John Allan the elder was apparently living when he applied for burgess rights in Stirling.

The blade is of a type continuously made for export to Scotland until the 19th century.

This is traditionally the sword surrendered by George Mackenzie, 3rd Earl of Cromartie, on the day before the Battle of Culloden, a military detachment under Capt Reay Mackay having surprised him at dinner at Dunrobin. The Earl was subsequently pardoned.

Lender: Geoffrey Jenkinson.

1 Whitelaw, in *Transactions*, pp 24-7.

2 Whitelaw, *Scottish Arms Makers*, pp 215 and 282-3.

3 Rolland, p 20.

1:14 Basket-hilted backsword (claidheamh cùil)

Hilt, Scottish (Stirling), probably first quarter 18th century; blade, German (Solingen), 17th-century.

The iron hilt consists of a pommel and a basket very similar to that of 1:13, except that, apart from the shields, the inlay consists only of interlace. Each of the shields bears a five-pointed star set around with 'cup-and ring' marks. The edges of the broader guards are cut with pairs of claw-like merlons at the centre and at each end. The same signature occurs on the quillon as on 1:13.

The grip is covered with grey rayskin and bound with silver foil. Silver ferrules edged with scallops and points alternating. The three-quarter liner is of buff leather covered with red cloth. The fringe is of crimson and green wool.

The straight, one-edged blade is struck on the outer face between two 'sickle' marks with JACOB/BRACH, and on the inner face MEFECIT/SOLINGEN.

Length overall, 38$^{5}/_{16}$".

A man named Jacob Brach 'zu Bavert' was sworn into the Solingen Guild of Swordcutlers in 1640.[1]

Lender: The Duke of Atholl (Blair Castle).

1 Weyersberg, p 15.

1:15 Basket-hilted backsword (claidheamh cùil)

Hilt, Scottish (Stirling?), second quarter 18th century; blade, probably German and contemporary with the hilt.

The iron hilt is similar to that of 1:13, except that the wrist-guard is smaller. The edges of the broad guards are mainly cut with fishtail merlons alternating with obtuse points. The piercing includes rather elongated 'hearts' with a small spike projecting below each lobe. On the shields the corner holes are also heart-shaped. Stamped on the rear quillon towards the hand are the letters WA. The ends of the knuckle-guards are now soldered to a pommel-ring.

The grip, liner and scabbard are all 19th-century.

The straight, one-edged blade has two narrow contiguous fullers. Stamped in both fullers on each face is X ANDRIA X FARARA.

Length overall, 37$^{1}/_{2}$".

The absence from the maker's signature of a letter signifying the name of the town is probably due to a repair on the wrist-guard. The initials appear to be those identified as belonging to Walter Allan, armourer in Stirling, active *c*1732-1760.[1]

The addition of a pommel-ring gave greater stability to the basket.

Lender: Geoffrey Jenkinson.

1 See under 1:34.

1:16 Basket-hilted broadsword (claidheamh mòr)

Hilt, Scottish, perhaps first quarter 18th century; blade, German (Solingen), probably contemporary with the hilt.

The iron hilt is similar to that of 1:13, except that the pommel is domed and that the ends of the knuckle-guards are only slightly indented. The wrist-guard is wide. The edges of the broad guards are cut with truncated obtuse points and fishtail merlons. The piercing includes 'hearts' in which the upper corners of the lower part project below the lobes.

The grip is modern.

The straight, two-edged blade has a ricasso, 2$^{3}/_{4}$" long, with a flute near each edge, and three separate narrow fullers, all starting at the hilt. Stamped in the fullers on each face in small letters is ME FECIT/HERMMEN KEISER/ SOLINGEN.

Length overall, 38$^{11}/_{16}$".

Although several blades signed by Herman Keiser are recorded, there is apparently no record of a man of this name in the Solingen archives.[1]

Lender: The National Trust for Scotland.

1 Weyersberg, p 25.

1:17 Basket-hilted broadsword (claidheamh mòr)

Hilt, Scottish, second quarter 18th century; blade, German (Solingen), probably contemporary with the hilt.

The iron hilt is similar to that of 1:13 except that ends of the knuckle-guards lack the flanking claws. (The wrist-guard is broken off.) The edges of the broad guards are all plain. The piercing includes 'hearts' like those on 1:16.

The grip has been re-covered with sheepskin over a spiral binding. Inside the basket are a piece of leather and a buff-leather fringe.

The blade is similar to that of 1:9.

Length overall, 38$^{1}/_{4}$".

Lender: Geoffrey Jenkinson.

1:18 *Basket-hilted backsword* (claidheamh cùil)

Hilt, Scottish, perhaps first quarter 18th century; blade, German (probably Solingen), after 1701.

The iron hilt consists of a pommel and a basket similar to that of 1:16. A broad, scrolled wrist-guard has been riveted on, either to replace one that had been broken off, or to improve a basket originally made without one. Only the side-guards are fluted. The edges of all the broader guards are cut with merlons, either fishtail or triple-pointed, scallops, and obtuse points. The piercing of the broader guards consists of 'hearts' like those of 1:11. On the shields the piercings at the centre and corners of the shields are quatrefoils.

The grip is covered with black skin from a dogfish and bound with twists of copper wire. The three-quarter liner is of buff leather covered with red cloth. The fringe is of crimson wool.

The straight, one-edged blade has a ricasso $1^{7}/_{16}$" long, a broad full-length fuller at the spine, starting at the ricasso, and a bevelled false edge $9^{1}/_{8}$" long. Etched and fire-gilt with a false-watered panel on the ricasso, and on the outer face with *God Save/King James/thee 8*, and on the other face with *Prosperity/to Schotlandt/and/no union*. Beyond this on the outer face is a male bust seen in profile, wearing a cap, and beyond that a crown over two sceptres, and on the inside *St: Andrias* and his cross.

The scabbard of black blind-tooled leather is a later replacement, but the two original belt-hooks have been re-used.

For blades with this inscription see Trenchard, pp 21-4.

Blades such as that of 1:17 and 1:26 were presumably intended for Scottish Jacobites for whom James was the eighth king of that name.

Traditionally this is the sword carried in 1715 at the Battle of Sheriffmuir by Donald Maclean of Torloisk, and in 1745 at the Battle of Prestonpans by Hector Maclean of Torloisk, each acting as major of the clan regiment.

Length overall, 40".

Lender: Captain Alwyn Compton Farquharson of Invercauld.

1:19 *Basket-hilted broadsword* (claidheamh mòr)

Hilt, Scottish, second quarter 18th century; blade, probably German and contemporary with the hilt.

The iron hilt is similar to that of 1:17. There is a broad, scrolled wrist-guard. The piercing includes 'hearts' like those on 1:30. All the broader guards are decorated with delicate rocker-work.

The grip has lost its cover. The piece of leather before the hand is shaped by use. There are the remains of a woollen fringe.

There are traces of an almost illegible inscription in the central fullers, possibly ANDRIA on the inner face, and FARARA on the outer.

Length overall, $38^{1}/_{16}$".

Lender: Bruce Mackie.

1:20 *Basket-hilted broadsword* (claidheamh mòr)

Hilt, Scottish, second quarter 18th century; blade, German (Solingen), probably contemporary with the hilt.

The iron hilt is generally similar to that of 1:13. The pommel is domed, the ends of the knuckle-guards lack the flanking claws, the shields are unusually small and the quillons are broader than customary. The part of the basket behind the main axis of the sword extends unusually far to the rear. The forward-guards are particularly prominent. The edges of the broad-guards are cut with a variety of relatively large scallops and cusps. The piercing includes 'hearts' like those of 1:17.

The grip is covered in brown leather.

Incised on the flat of the blade and inlaid in brass is the mark of a stylised wolf.

Length overall, $38^{3}/_{16}$".

Lender: Geoffrey Jenkinson.

1:21 *Basket-hilted backsword* (claidheamh cùil)

Hilt, Scottish, second quarter 18th century; blade, German (Solingen), probably late 17th century.

The iron hilt is generally similar to that of 1:17, but of normal proportions. The pommel is encompassed by complex mouldings. There is a broad, scrolled wrist-guard. The shields, which are quatrefoils, are supported by saltire-bars chiselled to resemble leaves emerging between the petals. The edges of the broad guards are bracket-cut with a small scallop at the centre. The piercing includes 'hearts' like those of 1:15, except that there is a fishtail merlon between the lobes.

The grip is covered with grey rayskin and bound at intervals with brass foil. Brass ferrules with scalloped edges. The fringe is of gold thread.

The straight blade, which is now one-edged, has a ricasso $1^{3}/_{8}$" long, and two separate fullers flanking the original central line. Etched in line with sprays of stylised foliage, the words [A]NDR[EA]/[F]ARA[A], written transversely, and the script letters L over L G.

Length overall, $38^{1}/_{8}$".

This hilt closely resembles that worn by James Moray of Abercairney in his portrait by Jeremiah Davison, painted about 1737.[1] It was quite common for old two-edged blades to be brought up to date by making them one-edged. It would be tempting to identify the initials on the blade as those of Lord Lewis Gordon, younger brother of the 3rd Duke of Gordon. At the time he joined the Prince in October, 1745 he was a serving officer in the Royal Navy. His elder brother Lord Charles Gordon held a commission in Loudoun's Regiment of Foot and unlike his brother stayed loyal to King George. Lord Lewis spent time in the north-east recruiting for the Prince.

Lender: Geoffrey Jenkinson.

1 Hesketh, Pl X.

1:22 *Basket-hilted backsword* (claidheamh cùil)

Hilt, Scottish (Stirling), about 1740; blade, of 17th-century type.

The silver hilt consists of a pommel and a basket of more or less conventional form with bars of circular section. The ends of the longitudinal guards are now riveted to a pommel-ring. The longitudinal guards are made in the form of elongated figures-of-eight, and the concave-sided shields are set at the centre of a quatrefoil outlined with bars. The terminal of the side-guard towards the blade, which is of conventional form, is balanced at the other end by a open heart between horns. The piercing of the shields includes a central quatrefoil, four stars of four points, and four 'hearts' like those of 1:11. The side-guard is pierced with a quatrefoil. The open-work wrist-guard is scrolled. Stuck on the rear quillon towards the hand are four marks: the letters CM within a rectangle (struck twice), the letter F, and a stag's head erased; the CM mark is also struck on the main knuckle-guard over the first finger. Struck on the rear quillon towards the blade with the letters W A over S.

The grip is covered with grey rayskin and bound with twists of silver wire. Silver ferrules with scalloped edges. The three-quarter liner of thin buff leather is covered in faded red velvet.

The straight, one-edged blade has a ricasso 2¼" long and two narrow fullers, starting at the hilt. Struck on each face is FERARA, flanked by pairs of 'sickle' marks.

The scabbard of black leather has two silver mounts. The belt-hook has been broken off.

Length overall, 38⁹⁄₁₆".

This is the sword preserved at Achnacarry as that of Donald Cameron of Lochiel, 19th Chief, who led the clan out in '45.

The mark on the knuckle-guard is that of Colin Mitchell, goldsmith in the Canongate (active 1727-53), from whom Walter Allan is known to have ordered the silver mountings for his swords.[1] The stag's-head mark is that of the Canongate silversmiths. The F is presumably some form of unofficial date-letter.

Lender: Sir Donald Cameron of Lochiel, Achnacarry.

1 S Maxwell, 'Letters from Walter Allan, Armourer in Stirling, to Colin Mitchell, Goldsmith in Canongate, 1741-1750', in Caldwell, pp 408-18, where the date-letter was read as an L.

Donald Cameron of Lochiel, by an unknown artist (c1740).

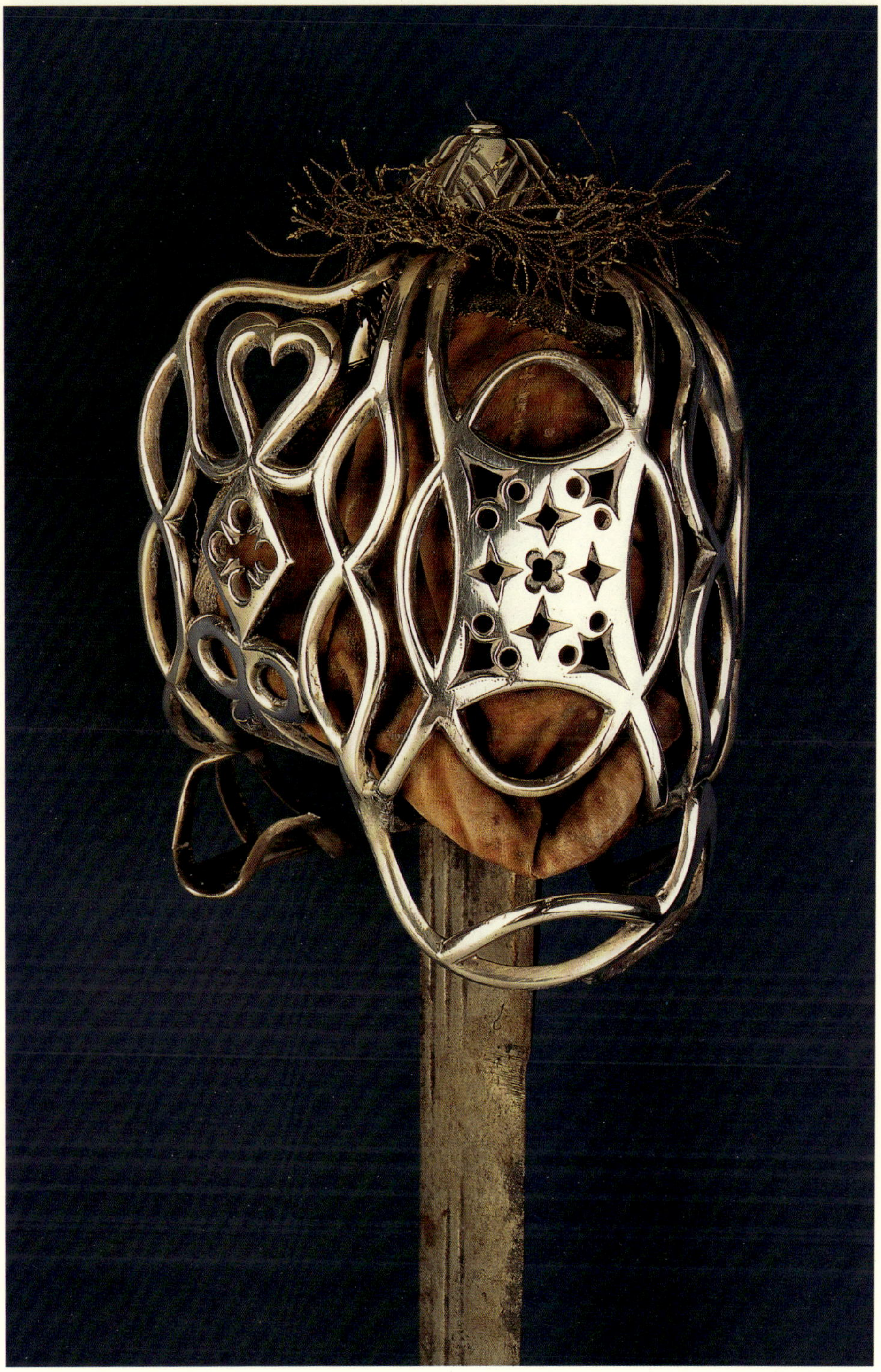

The next five swords have brass baskets of conventional design, but are of different construction to the iron hilts. With the exception of the forward-guards, the whole complex was cast flat and in one piece and was then bent round to enclose the hand. The joins were then brazed. The most obvious difference is that the end of the rear quillon, which projects slightly beyond the additional rear-guard, supports a cylindrical stud projecting towards the blade. The oblate pommel, which is sometimes octagonal in plan, has a tall narrow neck. In what are presumably the earlier examples, the ends of the knuckle-guards expand to partially encompass this neck. Item 1:24 is, and 1:23 has been, of this type. The bars are usually fluted longitudinally, and the edges of the broad guards are usually either waved or gently cusped and scalloped. The forward-guards, which are made of a V-shaped casting, usually meet the main knuckle-guard over the first finger. The piercing usually consists of T-shaped 'hearts', the cross-bar formed by two round holes and the vertical by a rectangle.

John Wallace originally dated this class of hilt about 1750-60, but he later tentatively redated them to about 1720.[1]

1 Wallace, p 54 & fig 45; personal communication, 1981.

1:23 Basket-hilted broadsword (claidheamh mòr)

Hilt, Scottish, probably about 1720; blade, probably German, of 17th-century type.

The brass hilt consists of a pommel of octagonal plan, and a basket of conventional form. Each facet of the pommel is engraved with a saltire. The ends of the knuckle-guards have been linked to a pommel-ring at a later date, to increase the stability of the hilt. The edges of the broad guards are wavy. The piercing includes 'hearts' similar to those of 1:22.

The grip is covered with black rayskin and bound at intervals with a twist of brass wire. The cotton fringe is later.

The straight two-edged blade, which is unsharpened for $5^{1}/_{2}$" at the hilt, is of lenticular section thereafter. It has three separate narrow fullers; stamped in each of the outer fullers is a row of Xs, and in the central fuller on the outer face FERARA, and on the inner one ANDRI[A].

Length overall, $36^{15}/_{16}$".

Lender: Geoffrey Jenkinson.

1:24 Basket-hilted broadsword (claidheamh mòr)

Hilt, Scottish, probably about 1720; blade, probably German, of 17th-century type.

The gilt-brass hilt consists of a pommel of circular plan, its top encompassed by three concentric flutes, and a basket like that of 1:23, except that the ends of the knuckle-guards are not linked, and the edge of the 'ram's horns' towards the pommel is straight. The basket is not raked.

The grip and silk fringe are modern.

Stamped in the fuller on the outer face with FERARA SAHAGVN, and on the inner face with FERARA ELVIEHO. The inscription appears to have been altered at some time.

Length overall, $39^{7}/_{32}$".

What little is known at present about Alonzo de Sahagun the elder (*el vieho*), the Toledo swordsmith alive in 1571, will be found in *Wallace Collection Catalogues* pp 118-9. In this case the inscription is probably a contemporary forgery intended to impress the tyro swordsman.

This sword is traditionally that of one of the Murrays of Cringletie in Peeblesshire.

Lender: Geoffrey Jenkinson.

1:25 Basket-hilted backsword (claidheamh cùil)

Hilt, Scottish, probably about 1725; blade, German (probably Solingen) after 1701.

The brass hilt is very similar to that of 1:24, except that the pommel is plain; the ends of the two side knuckle-guards touch the main one but not each other; and the projection of the rear quillon ends in a simulated roll. The edges of the broader guards are cut with pairs of cusps alternating with either obtuse points or scallops. The grip is covered with white rayskin and bound at intervals with gilt foil. Gilt ferrules with scalloped edges. The three-quarter liner of buff leather is covered with red cloth.

The straight one-edged blade has a shoulder $^{1}/_{16}$" long, a broad full-length fuller at the spine and a false edge $8^{1}/_{4}$" long. Etched and fire-gilt with a false-watered panel, and on the outer face with the words *Vivat/Jacobus/tertius/magna/ Britarmia* [sic]/*Rex As*, and on the inside with *With this/ Good sword/thÿ Cause/I will maintain/and for thÿ/Sake O James/will breath/each vien* [sic]. Beyond, on each face, is the figure of a king.

Length overall, $39^{5}/_{8}$".

For blades with this inscription, see Trenchard, pp 6-8. Blades such as that of 1:25 were presumably intended for English Jacobites for whom James was the third king of that name.

Lender: Geoffrey Jenkinson.

1:26 One-edged blade

German (probably Solingen), after 1701.

Similar to the blade of 1:25, except that there is a ricasso, 1 7/8" long, at the end of which the fuller commences. The false edge is 8 1/2" long. About 1" has been broken from the point. The inscription on the outer face reads *Prosperity/To/Schotland/and /No Union*, and that on the inner face, *God Save/King James/The 8*. Beyond this is etched on the outer face St Andrew (*St Andreas*) with his cross, and on the inner face a laurelled male bust and a crown and sceptre on a cushion.

Length overall, 39".

For blades with this inscription see Trenchard, pp.21-4.

Blades such as this were presumably intended for Scottish Jacobites for whom James was the eighth king of that name.

Lender: Geoffrey Jenkinson.

1:27 Basket-hilted broadsword (claidheamh mòr)

Hilt, Scottish, probably about 1730; blade, German (Saxon), early 18th century.

The brass hilt is very similar to that of 1:23, except that the pommel is plain, and the ends of the knuckle-guards are joined to a pommel-ring.

The grip has been re-covered in sheepskin.

Etched in blackened line near the hilt with the letters AR crowned, the cipher of Augustus I, 'the Strong', Elector of Saxony, as King of Poland (1697-1733).

Length overall, 41 1/8".

Lender: Geoffrey Jenkinson

1:28 Basket-hilted broadsword (claidheamh mòr)

Hilt, Scottish, probably about 1720; blade, probably German and contemporary with the hilt.

The brass hilt is very similar to that of 1:23, except that the pommel is circular in plan, and the guards are not fluted. The ends of the knuckle-guards are not expanded and simply abut on the neck of the pommel. The basket is not raked.

The grip is covered with white rayskin and bound at intervals with gilt wire. Gilt ferrules with scalloped edges. The piece of buff leather inside the basket is covered with red velvet.

Stamped in the central fuller on each face with ANDREIA FARARA, and with a pair of addorsed 'sickle marks' between the words.The wooden scabbard, which is covered with brown leather, has a brass mouthpiece with a scalloped edge. The independent belt-hook and the crampet are now missing.

Length overall, 38 1/4".

Lender: Geoffrey Jenkinson.

The hilts of the next two swords differ from the classic Highland basket-hilt only in that in place of the longitudinal element of the side-guard, there is an S-shaped bar linking the centre points of the side knuckle-guard and the rear-guard.

The hilts of the following three swords differ from the classic Highland basket-hilt principally in that their main longitudinal guards arise on an oval plate through the centre of which the tang passes, rather than on a conventional pair of quillons.

All three come from the collection of George IV and are recorded in the catalogue of Carlton House, his London residence, as Nos 3142, 3143 and 3149. They had previously belonged to George III and, after his death in 1822, were transferred to Carlton House.

1:29 Basket-hilted broadsword (claidheamh mòr)

Hilt, Scottish, probably early 18th-century; blade, probably German and early 17th-century.

The iron hilt consists of a large domed pommel with a step for the ends of the guards, and a basket of fully-developed Highland type with stout bars of circular section. The transverse edges of the shields are cut with a single pair of fishtail merlons flanking a small U-shaped inlet. The other edges of the broad-guards are all cut like those of 1:7. The piercing includes 'hearts' made up of three separate holes, one triangular with a small point projecting between two round ones.

The grip lacks its cover. The liner is later.

Crudely struck in the fuller on each face, in large letters is ANDREIA XX FARARA XX. The point has been broken off.

Length overall, 39 7/16".

Lender: Geoffrey Jenkinson.

1:30 Basket-hilted broadsword (claidheamh mòr)

Hilt, Scottish, probably early 18th-century; blade, probably German and early 17th-century.

The iron hilt consists of a large pommel, and a basket generally similar to that of 1:29. (The present wrist-guard is a 19th-century replacement.) The transverse edges of the shields are cut with a single pair of fishtail merlons flanking a pair of scallops, and the longitudinal edges with U-shaped openings, obtuse points and scallops, all flanked by similar merlons. The other edges of the broader guards are all cut like those of 1:7. The piercing includes 'hearts' with a deep inlet under each lobe. The holes at the centre and corners of the shields are quatrefoil. The broader guards are engraved with 'cup-and-ring' marks, and the fluting is picked out with rocker-work.

The grip is covered with black fishskin and bound at intervals with brass wire. The liner and silk fringe are later.

The straight, two-edged blade, which is of lenticular section, is very worn. Stamped in each fuller on the inner face is [AND]RIA XX.

Length overall, 38 5/16".

Lender: Geoffrey Jenkinson.

WILLIAM AUGUSTUS DUKE OF CUMBERLAND

1:31 Basket-hilted broadsword (claidheamh mòr)

Hilt, Scottish (Elgin), about 1713; blade, German (Solingen), probably early 18th-century.

The silver hilt consists of a barrel-shaped pommel and a basket of more or less conventional form with bars of flattened-oval section. The lobated end of each of the knuckle-guards is screwed to the pommel. The rounded end of the rear quillon, which projects slightly beyond the basket, is turned towards the blade. The side-guards each consist of a broad strip of silver sheet cut and engraved with the upper part of a fleur-de-lis at the end towards the blade, with an applied longitudinal ridge crudely shaped like a stylised worm or caterpillar. The shields each consist of an heraldic shield beneath a closed crown of five arches. The inner shield bears the initals C R in a foliate script linked by a small saltire, and the outer shield a thistle slipped between two number Is. On each side bridging the gap between the two saltire bars towards the blade is a narrow strip of silver, that on the inner face engraved *praemium hoc ab illomo. dño Alēxro/Marchione: de Huntly oblatum*, and that on the outer face *quod adeptus est Geo: Gordon de Gleshrin/haeredibus suis transmitti jubet*. The broad main knuckle-guard, which has a knurled edge, is engraved *Win* at King Charles fair at Huntly Castell the secund/Tusday of september 1713 all horsess not Excsiding ane hundred/Markes of price ar admited to rune the rideres staking/Crounes a peace. Which ar giuin to the poor who may/Pray that ye Monarchie and Royall family my be Lasting/And glorious in thes kingdomes*. Struck on the main knuckle-guard are three punches, 1) the capital letters V S conjoined in a square, 2) the word ELGIN in a rectangle with rounded corners, and 3) the capital letter D in a shield-shaped punch. The forward-guards are vestigial.

The barrel-shaped, silver grip is spirally bound at intervals with silver wire. Silver ferrules.

The straight, two-edged blade is of flattened-lenticular section, with a ricasso, $1^{1}/_{4}$" long, with a flute near each edge and a shallow hollow at its centre.

Length overall, $40^{1}/_{2}$".

It is possible that 1:31 is one of two silver basket-hilted swords in the post-mortem inventory of the Duke of Cumberland.[1] The Duke's collection passed to George III.

The winner of this sword, George Gordon of Glastiren in Banffshire, was out in '15. If 1:31 was subsequently in the collection of the Duke of Cumberland, it had presumably been taken in the aftermath of Culloden.

The maker of the hilt was William Scott II, who became a burgess of Aberdeen in 1691, worked at first in that city, but later in Banff (from about 1699), and traded in Elgin from 1701. He died in 1748.[2] An earlier and rather more elaborate version of this type of hilt, given for the race in 1701, is now in the Museum of Antiquities, Edinburgh.[3] It bears the same maker's mark, but this appears to have been used also by William Scott I (active 1666-*c*1702). The prizes, whether in the form of a sword or a cup, were valued at £10 Scots. The initials on the inner shield stand for *Carolus Rex*, and the two uprights on the outer shell probably stand for II (*secundus*), but might represent a capital H, for Huntly, its cross-bar concealed by the thistle.[4]

Lent by Her Majesty The Queen.

1 Cumberland Papers, Vol 1, p 63.

2 James, pp 41-2.

3 J P How, 'The Huntly Race and its Trophies' in O'Connor & Clarke, which gives the history of this race and points out the strong Jacobite connections in the design of the hilt; see especially pp 494-6, fig 213.

4 P J Lankester, pp 271-2.

Literature: Campbell, Pl 12; Laking, *Armoury of Windsor Castle* No.756; Finlay, *Highland Weapons* Pl.1.

1:32 Basket-hilted broadsword (claidheamh mòr)

Hilt, British (Old Aberdeen, Scotland), about 1727; blade, German (Solingen), possibly second half 17th century.

The silver hilt is generally similar in form to that of 1:31 except that there are no inscribed strips linking the saltire bars, and that the side-guard consists of a bar of flattened-oval section with its terminal cast and chased as a fleur-de-lis. The part of the rear quillon which projects beyond the basket is cast and chased in the form of a fleur-de-lis. The broad main knuckle-guard, which has a knurled edge, is engraved: *Given by the Duke of Gordon and Winn at Huntly Castle the/ second Thursday of Septr 1727 years all Horses not exceeding 13 hands/ and 2 inches high are admitted to runn and the winning Horse to be sold/ for ane Hundred merks if required by the Judge of the Race. The/ Riders staiking Crouns a piece which are given to the Poor to/ pray that the Monarchy and Royal Family may be lasting and/ Glorious in these Kingdoms.*

Struck on the stool towards the blade with four marks, 1) a closed crown within an oval, 2) the capital letters R C in a rectangle, 3) the capital letters OABD (A and B conjoined) in a rectangle with rounded ends, 4) the capital letter C in a rectangle with cut corners.

The grip is like that of 1:31. The buff-leather liner is covered with red cloth. There is also a removable leather oval in front of the hand.

The straight, two-edged blade is of lenticular section, with a ricasso, approximately $2^{5}/_{8}$" long, and three narrow contiguous fullers. The flutes and fullers all bear traces of fire-gilding. Struck in the central fuller is XX ANDRIA X FARARA XX. Struck on each face of the ricasso with a circular punch framing the capital letters C B conjoined.

Length overall, $39^{7}/_{16}$".

It is possible that 1:32 is the 'Silver Do [ie basket-hilted sword] gilt blade' of the post-mortem inventory of the Duke of Cumberland,[1] whose collection passed to George III.

The maker of the hilt of 1:32 was the silversmith Robert Cruickshank of Old Aberdeen, who was recorded from 1699 to 1731.[2]

The mark on the blade may be one used by Clemens Botter, a Solingen blade-smith recorded in 1685.[3]

Not exhibited. Photograph The Royal Collection © Her Majesty The Queen.

1 Cumberland Papers, Vol 1, p 63.

2 James, pp 53-4, & J P How, 'The Huntly Race and its Trophies' in Connor & Clarke, pp 497-8.

3 Letter of Dr A-H Haedeke, 16.V.1990.

Literature: Item 1:32 or a sword with a very similar hilt, is illustrated in Anderson & Drummond, Pl X, fig 3; Campbell, Pl 10; Laking, *Armoury of Windsor Castle* No 758, Pl 32 facing p 220; How, op cit, pp 497-8, fig 215; Finlay, *Scottish Gold and Silver Work* p 155; Finlay, 2nd edn, p 187; Lankester, pp 271-5, Pl 2a & 2b.

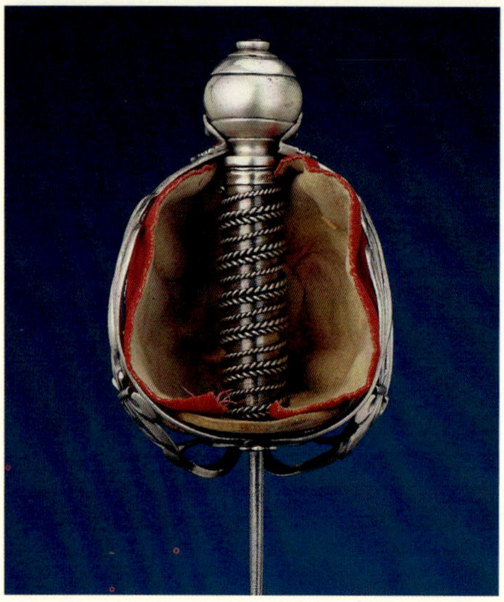

DUKE OF CUMBERLAND: ENGRAVING AFTER A POND

1:33 Basket-hilted backsword (claidheamh cùil)

Hilt, Scottish (possibly from the north-east), about 1730; blade, German (probably Solingen), late 17th-century.

The silver hilt consists of a large, low-domed pommel with a step for the ends of the guards, decorated with four radial petals in low relief, and a basket similar in form to that of 1:31 except that its unusually broad bars are of flattened-rectangular section, each with a longitudinal flute flanked on each side by two narrow ribs. The end of each of the knuckle-guards abuts on the pommel. There is an integral wrist-guard, with a closed scroll towards the blade, but no additional rear-guards. The side-guards, which have broad, central sections with a central longitudinal flute between two ridges, have fleur-de-lis terminals like those of 1:32. The outer shield differs in that the thistle is between the two letters I (or J) R. The main knuckle-guard has a broad, oval central section with cusped and scrolled edges. The rather prominent forward-guards continue the line of the side knuckle-guard in the manner of Stirling-made hilts.

The grip is covered with grey rayskin and bound at intervals with silver foil. Within the basket in front of the hand is a piece of thick buff leather. The sword-knot and tassel are of plain buff leather.

The straight, one-edged blade, has a ricasso 1³/₁₆" long, and two narrow, contiguous fullers. The false edge is approximately 7¹/₄" long. Etched in line on each face transversely with the name *Andrea/farara*, and with wiry foliate scrolls and stylised flowers.

Length overall, 37⁷/₈".

It is possible that 1:33 is one of two swords with silver basket-hilts in the post-mortem inventory of the Duke of Cumberland (see under 1:31).

There is no sign of any inscription having been removed from the main knuckle-guard. The letter R in the outer shield appears to be original. The combination IR presumably stands for *Jacobus rex*, referring to the Jacobite claimant, James III & VIII (1688-1766).[1]

A silver hilt of very similar appearance, but of conventional construction, is at Dunvegan in Skye, and is shown in Allan Ramsay's portrait of Norman, 22nd Chief of MacLeod, painted in 1746.

The basket bears the Edinburgh marks for 1728/9.[2] It is, however, constructed in the same way as conventional baskets instead of with an oval stool. The prize for the Huntly Fair race in the years 1731 to 1734 was a silver-hilted sword. The first two were made by James Taitt and the remainder by William Aytoune, both Edinburgh goldsmiths.[3]

Etching of this type occurs on a blade in the Tøjhusmuseum, Copenhagen, dated 1650,[4] and on another in Paris, dated either 1651 or 1657.[5]

Sword-knots are rare on Highland swords but one is illustrated in Allan Ramsay's portrait of John Campbell, 4th Earl of Loudoun, painted in the uniform of his Highland regiment.[6] See also 1:42.

Lent by Her Majesty The Queen.

1 Lankester, p 273.

2 Lankester, pp 277-82, Pls 6, & 7a-c.

3 How, 'The Huntly Race and its Trophies' in O'Connor & Clarke, pp 498-9.

4 Cat No C290/42.

5 Musée de l'Armée, Inv No J Po 1571.

6 Property of the Marquess of Bute (Munro, illus p 46).

Literature: Laking, *Armoury of Windsor Castle* No 754, Pl 32, facing p 220; Finlay, 2nd edn, p 152; Lankester, pp 271-6, Pls 4a-b.

Basket-hilts of Stirling type

Although basket-hilts of conventional type were made and signed by Stirling armourers,[1] the burgh is better known for its elaborately decorated hilts. In these the area between the side knuckle-guards is filled with a screen of bars more or less fancifully arranged; the area between the pommel and this screen on each side of the main knuckle-guard is partially filled by a small triangular guard; and the ends of the longitudinal guards are welded to a ring which encompasses the neck of the pommel. The forward-guards, which project over the blade rather than forward, curve round to continue the line of the side knuckle-guard. They are often bridged by a silver ornament, or are partially or wholly filled by a bar or plate. In many examples both ends of the side-guard are made to match.

The inventor of this type of hilt is thought to be Walter Allan, who was admitted freeman of the Incorporation of Hammermen of Stirling in 1732.[2]

1 For instance the hilt in the Museum of Antiquities, Edinburgh, inscribed 'John Allan Stirling 1716' (Inv No LA22; Wallace, Pls 33-4), and 1:13 & 1:15 above.

2 Reid, in *Scottish Art Review*, pp 16-21 & 37.

1:34 Basket-hilted backsword (claidheamh cùil)

Hilt, Scottish (Stirling), probably about 1735-40; blade, German or Scottish, and probably contemporary with the hilt.

The iron hilt, decorated with brass, consists of a biconical pommel with a deep equatorial groove for the ends of the guards, and a basket of characteristic Stirling type (except that it lacks a pommel-ring), with bars of rectangular section each with a longitudinal flute between two narrow, rocker-work grooves. The additional rear-guards are longer than the main rear-guards. A wide, brass wrist-guard, which is riveted on, is stamped with the letters W A over S. The side-guards, which have straight 'ram's horns' with ends shaped like arrow-heads, each has a heart-shaped terminal pierced by a very narrow 'heart' with a small blunt point between its lobes and a larger point below each lobe. The area in front of the fingers between the side knuckle-guards is filled by a grille of longitudinal bars, three on each side of the main knuckle-guard. The central bar of each trio, the main knuckle-guard and the side-guards, which are wavy and pierced with acutely pointed 'hearts', are overlaid with brass.

Inside the hilt is a piece of thick leather covered with pink velvet, and a fringe of silver thread.

The grip is covered with grey rayskin and bound at intervals with silver foil. Silver ferrules.

The straight, one-edged blade, has a ricasso 1" long, a narrow fuller close to the spine, and a false edge 9" long. Stamped on the flat on each face is a quatrefoil made with a C-shaped punch and with a straight one for the diagonals. Stamped on each face of the ricasso is a circle with four dots equally spaced about its edge, and in each fuller ANDRIA FERARA.

Length overall, 39 7/16".

The catalogue of the Armoury of George IV records that 1:34 was received in March 1822 from the collection of George III (No 3146). Possibly the 'Iron basket hilt brass Ornaments' of the post-mortem inventory of the Duke of Cumberland,[1] whose collection passed to George III.

The initials on the wrist-guard have been identified as those of Walter Allan, armourer and swordcutler in Stirling, admitted a freeman of the Incorporation of Hammermen of the burgh in 1732. He died in 1761.[2] The absence of a pommel-ring probably indicates that 1:34 is a precursor of his fully-developed hilt. If it did belong to the Duke of Cumberland, it probably would have been acquired in the aftermath of Culloden.

Lent by Her Majesty The Queen

1 Cumberland Papers, Vol 1, p.63.

2 Whitelaw, in *Transactions*, p 283; S Maxwell, 'Letters from Walter Allan', in Caldwell, p 408.

Literature: Laking, *Armoury of Windsor Castle*, No 757, Pl 32, facing p 220; Reid, in *Scottish Art Review*, pp 19-20, Pl 7.

1:35 Basket-hilted backsword (claidheamh cùil)

Hilt, Scottish (Stirling), second quarter 18th century; blade, probably German and contemporary with the hilt.

Hilt of iron consisting of a pommel, and a basket generally similar to that of 1:34, except that the ends of the knuckle-guards are united with a pommel-ring, the screen of longitudinal bars is crossed by a central transverse bar, and the ends of the side-guards are symmetrical; each end having a pierced heart-shaped terminal flanked by horns. The edges of all the main bars are waved. The surface is decorated all over with rocker-work. The area within each of the forward-guards is bridged by a crowned thistle slipped in engraved silver. The junction of the forward guards is covered by a smaller thistle. Struck on the rear quillon towards the blade are the letters W A over S.

The grip is covered with white rayskin and bound at intervals with silver foil and wire twists. Silver ferrules with scalloped edges. The fringe is of gold thread.

The straight, one-edged blade has a narrow fuller, along the leading edge of which is engraved a series of scallops. Stamped in the fuller is X ANDRIA X FARARA X.

Length overall, $37^{25}/_{32}$".

For the maker of this hilt, see under 1:34. This type of blade was often mounted in Stirling hilts.

Lender: Geoffrey Jenkinson.

Literature: Reid, in *Scottish Art Review*, pp 19-20, Pl 3.

1:36 Basket-hilted backsword (claidheamh cùil)

Hilt, Scottish (Stirling), second quarter 18th century; blade, probably German and contemporary with the hilt.

Hilt of iron consisting of a pommel, and a basket generally similar to that of 1:35 except that the main bars are not waved and are longitudinally fluted, the bars of the screen are alternately straight and wavy, and the ends of the side-guards are not symmetrical. (The applied silver decoration of the forward-guard is missing.) Struck on the rear quillon are the letters W A over S.

The grip and liner are later.

The straight, one-edged blade has two contiguous fullers. Stamped in the broader fuller in large letters is ANDREA FERARA. Incised at each end of the inscription is an imperial orb.

Length overall, $38^{21}/_{32}$".

For the maker of this hilt, see under 1:34.

Lender: Geoffrey Jenkinson.

1:37 Basket-hilted broadsword (claidheamh mòr)

Hilt, Scottish (Stirling), second quarter 18th century; blade, probably German and contemporary with the hilt.

Hilt of iron consisting of an associated pommel, a basket generally similar to that of 1:35, except that the screen is made up of bars outlining 'hearts', the four main ones arranged point to point to form a cross, with smaller 'hearts' filling all the spaces. (The wrist-guard is a replacement.) Struck on the rear quillon with the letters W A: presumably the S was obliterated by the rivet of the new wrist-guard.

The grip is covered with black skin from a dogfish, and bound at intervals with twists of gilt wire. The three-quarter liner of buff leather is partly covered with red cloth. The fringe is of green and red wool.

The straight, two-edged blade has a ricasso, $1^{1}/_{2}$" long, and a narrow fuller near the spine, and a false edge $8^{1}/_{2}$" long. Stamped in the fuller is X ANDRIA X FARARA X.

Length overall, $38^{5}/_{32}$".

For the maker of this hilt, see under 1:34.

Lender: Geoffrey Jenkinson.

1:38 *Basket-hilted broadsword* (claidheamh mòr)

Hilt, Scottish (Stirling), second quarter 18th century; blade, probably German, late 17th century.

Hilt of iron very similar to that of 1:35, except that the pommel is conical, the bars of the basket are a little stouter, and the fillers within the forward-guards are pierced diamonds of steel. Stamped on the rear quillon towards the blade are G over a smaller s. The G may have been preceded by another letter, perhaps poorly struck, now worn away.

The grip is similar to that of 1:35, but the cover is of black dogfish skin. The three-quarter liner is of buff leather covered in red cloth. The later fringe is of crimson cotton.

The very worn, straight, two-edged blade has a ricasso and two central fullers, starting at the ricasso. There are traces of etched foliage. Struck on each face of the ricasso is the same mark as on 1:9, but in each case the fourth quarter cannot be read.

The scabbard is similar to that of 1:17.

Length overall, $38^{3}/_{4}$".

The initials on the hilt are probably those of James Grant, armourer in Stirling, who was admitted as burgess on 5 May 1759 (Whitelaw, *Scottish Arms Makers*, p 283).

Lender: Captain Alwyne Compton Farquharson of Invercauld.

1:39 *Basket-hilted backsword* (claidheamh cùil)

Hilt, Scottish (Stirling), second quarter 18th century; blade, German (Solingen) of 17th-century type.

Hilt of iron consisting of a pommel of trefoliate plan, a basket generally similar to that of 1:37, except that the screen consists of a reticulated pattern of narrow bars.

The grip, which is covered with grey skin from a dogfish, lacks its binding. The three-quarter liner of buff leather is covered with red cloth.

The straight, one-edged blade has a ricasso $4^{1}/_{4}$" long, and two separate narrow fullers, and a false edge $9^{1}/_{2}$" long. Struck on each face of the ricasso is the mark of a blackamoor's head viewed from his left. Stamped in the fullers on each face in letters of Spanish type is

** S * S ** ANDREA ** S * S *
** S * S ** FARARA ** S * S **

Length overall, $39^{15}/_{16}$".

At the time when this blade was probably made, this maker's mark was used by Peter Wundes, who was recorded in the Register of Solingen Swordcutlers in 1685.[1]

Lender: Geoffrey Jenkinson.

1 Letter of Dr A-H Haedeke, 16.V.1990.

1:40 *Basket-hilted backsword* (claidheamh cùil)

Hilt, Scottish (Stirling), second quarter 18th century; blade, probably German and contemporary with the hilt.

Hilt of iron, consisting of a pommel and a basket generally like that of 1:35, except that the side-guard is of the type usually found on the conventional Highland hilt. The screen consists of two trios of longitudinal bars flanking the main knuckle-guard, each pierced by longitudinal slots. The piercing includes 'hearts' like those of 1:15, but with a third spike between the lobes. The longitudinal piercings include long slots with pomy ends and edges cut with fishtail merlons, cusps, and U-shaped inlets.

The grip is covered with grey fishskin bounds with twists of brass wire. The three-quarter liner of buff leather is partly covered with red cloth.

The blade is similar to that of 1:35. It has a ricasso $2^{1}/_{4}$" long, a fuller $24^{1}/_{2}$" long, and a false edge 8" long.

Length overall, $39^{13}/_{32}$".

Lender: Geoffrey Jenkinson

The hilts of the next two swords are part of a group clearly strongly influenced by Stirling, but the place of their manufacture is not at present known. The feature which all have in common, but which does not appear to be found on hilts signed by Stirling makers, is a small triangular plate welded to the forward quillon on the face towards the blade. This supports two curved branches, each of which partially fill the area within one of the forward-guards.

1:41 Basket-hilted broadsword (claidheamh mòr)

Hilt, Scottish, probably second quarter 18th century; blade, probably German, possibly contemporary with the hilt.

Hilt of iron consisting of a pommel, and a basket generally like that of 1:35, except that the main bars are longitudinally fluted, and the ends of the side-guard are not symmetrical. The wide and tightly scrolled wrist-guard is either a later addition or a replacement. Each of the characteristic curved bars within the forward-guards is pierced with a hole like a double-ended heart.

The grip is covered with black skin from a dogfish. Silver ferrules with scalloped edges. Full liner of leather covered with red cloth.

The straight, two-edged blade has three narrow, separate fullers. Stamped in the outer fullers on each face with a series of circles some with a dot in the centre, and in the central fuller with XX ANDREA XX FERARA XX.

Length overall, 38 1/8".

Lender: Geoffrey Jenkinson.

1:42 Basket-hilted backsword (claidheamh cùil)

Hilt, Scottish, second quarter 18th century; blade, probably German, 17th century.

Hilt of iron, consisting of a pommel, and a basket generally like that of 1:41, except that the screen consists of longitudinal bars with wavy edges and piercing. The squares at each end of these bars are pierced with quatrefoils. The side-guards are of conventional form except that they have straight 'ram's horns'. Each of the characteristic curved bars within the forward-guards has wavy edges and wavy piercing.

The grip is covered with white rayskin and bound at intervals with twists of gilt wire. Turk's-head ferrules. Three-quarter liner of buff leather. Buff-leather sword-knot.

The straight, one-edged blade has a ricasso 1 5/8" long, and three contiguous fullers, all starting at the hilt, and a false edge 7" long. Stamped in the outer fullers on each face is W W W; in the central fuller on the outer face FARARA, and on the inner face ANDRIA.

Length overall, 40 15/16".

For the sword-knot, see under 1:33.

Lender: Geoffrey Jenkinson.

Basket-hilts made up of ribbon-like bars

A third type of basket-hilt was developed in parallel with the conventional type. Its characteristics are its very broad, ribbon-like guards. These are arranged as in the conventional basket, except that the shields are circular, there are no forward-guards, and in addition there is a small triangular guard linking the two saltire-bars towards the pommel and another those towards the blade. In some early examples the knuckle-guards each intersect a complex of guards shaped like a figure of eight (see 1:43 and 1:44). Some have a pair of long recurved quillons, but the later ones have only a very slight projection of the forward quillon and none at all at the rear. In later examples the ends of the knuckle-guards are welded to a three-quarter circle which clasps the front and sides of the pommel, and there is a narrow additional rear-guard (see 1:44 and 1:45). A few such hilts are signed with an initial or initials, but so far none has been satisfactorily identified (cf 1:44). Only one contemporary illustration of this type of hilt seems to be known; the portrait by Michael Wright of Sir Mungo Murray, painted about 1683.[1]

1 Scottish National Portrait Gallery, Edinburgh, Reg No PG 997.

1:43 Basket-hilted broadsword (claidheamh mòr)

Hilt, Scottish, possibly mid-17th century; blade, possibly early 18th century or earlier.

Hilt of iron consisting of a pommel (associated), and a 'ribbon' basket of the type in which each knuckle-guard bisects a guard shaped like a figure-of-eight. There is a pair of short, recurved extensions of the quillons beyond the perimeter of the basket. The area between the saltire-bars towards the blade is drop-shaped. The bars forming the triangular guard towards the pommel are themselves crossed in saltire. The ends of the knuckle-guards each fit into a slot in the pommel. A pair of small, blunt langets flanks the blade.

The grip now lacks its cover.

The blade is similar to that of 1:9, except that the mark of the king's head was made with a different punch, and the coat-of-arms occurs only on the outer face.

Length overall, 38¼".

A hilt of comparable construction was dated by Claude Blair 'early 17th century'.[1]

Lender: Geoffrey Jenkinson.

1 Blair, 'The early basket-hilt in Britain', in Caldwell, fig 123.

1:44 Basket-hilted broadsword (claidheamh mòr)

Hilt, Scottish, possibly mid-17th century; blade, possibly contemporary with the hilt.

Hilt of iron consisting of a pommel, and a 'ribbon' basket of the type with figure-of-eight guards, a short extension of the forward quillon, and thin additional rear-guards. The ends of the knuckle-guards each fit into a slot in the pommel. A pair of pointed langets flanks the blade.

The grip is covered with rayskin and bound with a twist of silver wire.

The straight, two-edged blade has a narrow central fuller.

Length overall 38¾".

Lender: Geoffrey Jenkinson.

1:45 Basket-hilted broadsword (claidheamh mòr)

Hilt, Scottish, probably last quarter 17th century; blade, French, contemporary with the hilt.

Hilt of iron consisting of a pommel, and a basket of the later 'ribbon' type in which the figure-of-eight guards are absent, both quillons project slightly beyond the perimeter of the basket, and there is a thin additional rear-guard. The ends of the knuckle-guards and of the triangular guards between the saltire-guards are all linked to a three-quarter pommel-ring. Struck on the quillon towards the blade are the letters TG in a rectangular punch.

The grip is covered with rayskin. There is a piece of leather in front of the hand.

The plain, straight, two-edged, hollow-ground blade is of flattened-hexagonal section for 9", and thereafter of diamond section. Inlaid in brass on the flat on the inner face is VIVE X LE X ROY X ET, and on the outer face, MON X SINNYOR X LE X DU.

Length overall, 41¼".

It is impossible to identify the maker of this hilt in the absence of any indication of where he worked. The blade is from a regulation sword of the French heavy cavalry.

Lender: Geoffrey Jenkinson.

1:46 Basket-hilted broadsword (claidheamh mòr)

Hilt, Scottish, probably last quarter 17th century; blade, German (Solingen), probably contemporary with the hilt.

Hilt of iron consisting of a pommel, and a basket similar to that of 1:45.

The grip is missing.

The straight, two-edged blade, which is of lenticular section, has a ricasso, $1\frac{7}{8}$" long, and three narrow separate fullers. Stamped in the outer fullers on each face is

** *SX*S* * SOLIDEO * *S*S* **
ANDREA FARARA
** *SX*S* * GLORIA * *S*S* **

Struck on each face of the ricasso is the same mark as on 1:37.

Length overall, $41\frac{3}{16}$".

Lender: Geoffrey Jenkinson.

Basket-hilts of unconventional form

1:47 Basket-hilted backsword (claidheamh cùil)

Hilt, of uncertain nationality and date, possibly Scottish and late 16th century.

The iron hilt consists of a pommel with a prominent tang-button, and a complicated basket of thin bars of rounded section. The basket is based on a pair of quillons supporting three knuckle-guards, two rear-guards, and two longitudinal guards, one on each face, lying between the main and the side knuckle-guards. Each of these guards is linked to its neighbours by a series of curved bars. The hole on each side of the rear quillon is partly filled by a curved bar projecting from the bar linking the forward ends of the side knuckle-guard and the rear-guard. The extension of the forward quillon has been broken off.

The grip is missing.

The straight, one-edged blade has a false edge 8" long.

Length overall, $41\frac{1}{2}$".

This very rare type of hilt was discussed by Claude Blair in 1981, when he knew only four examples, of which this was not one.[1] One of them, now in the National Museum, Dublin, had been found in County Cavan.

Lender: Geoffrey Jenkinson.

1 Blair, 'The early basket-hilt in Britain', in Caldwell, fig 134.

1:48 Basket-hilted horseman's broadsword (claidheamh mòr)

Hilt, Irish (Dublin), 1738/9; blade, probably German, of 17th-century type.

The silver hilt consists of a bun-pommel with a tang-button shaped like a cottage-loaf, and a basket very similar to the fully-developed Highland type, except that it is more spherical and it lacks the additional rear-guards. The rear quillon ends in a bun-shaped button. The forward-guards, which consist of a single Y-shaped plate soldered into place, project towards the blade. The bars, which are of flattened-rectangular section, are engraved with flowers and foliage. The outer shield is in the form of a small oval surrounded by four pairs of diverging scrolls. In place of the inner shield is an oval opening. Struck on each side knuckle-guard are three marks: Hibernia; a crowned harp; and the Gothic letter S; and on the end of each side-guard towards the blade is a small rectangular punch framing the letters WI.

The grip is of carved ebony.

The straight, two-edged blade has a ricasso, $2\frac{1}{4}$" long, with a flute at each edge, and three narrow fullers. Stamped on each face is

X XX SOLIDEO XX X
XX ANDRIA XX FARARA XX
X XX GLORIO XX X

Length overall, $41\frac{1}{2}$".

This sword may be the one lent by the Marquis of Breadalbane to the exhibition *Scottish National Memorials*, Bishop's Castle (see Paton, p 262 (No 1512)).

The first three silver marks were all used by the Dublin Assay office in the year 1738/9.[1] The maker's mark has not been identified.

Lender: Sir Donald Cameron of Lochiel, Achnacarry.

1 M J McAleer, *Dublin Silver Marks*, Appendix I in Pickford, p 742.

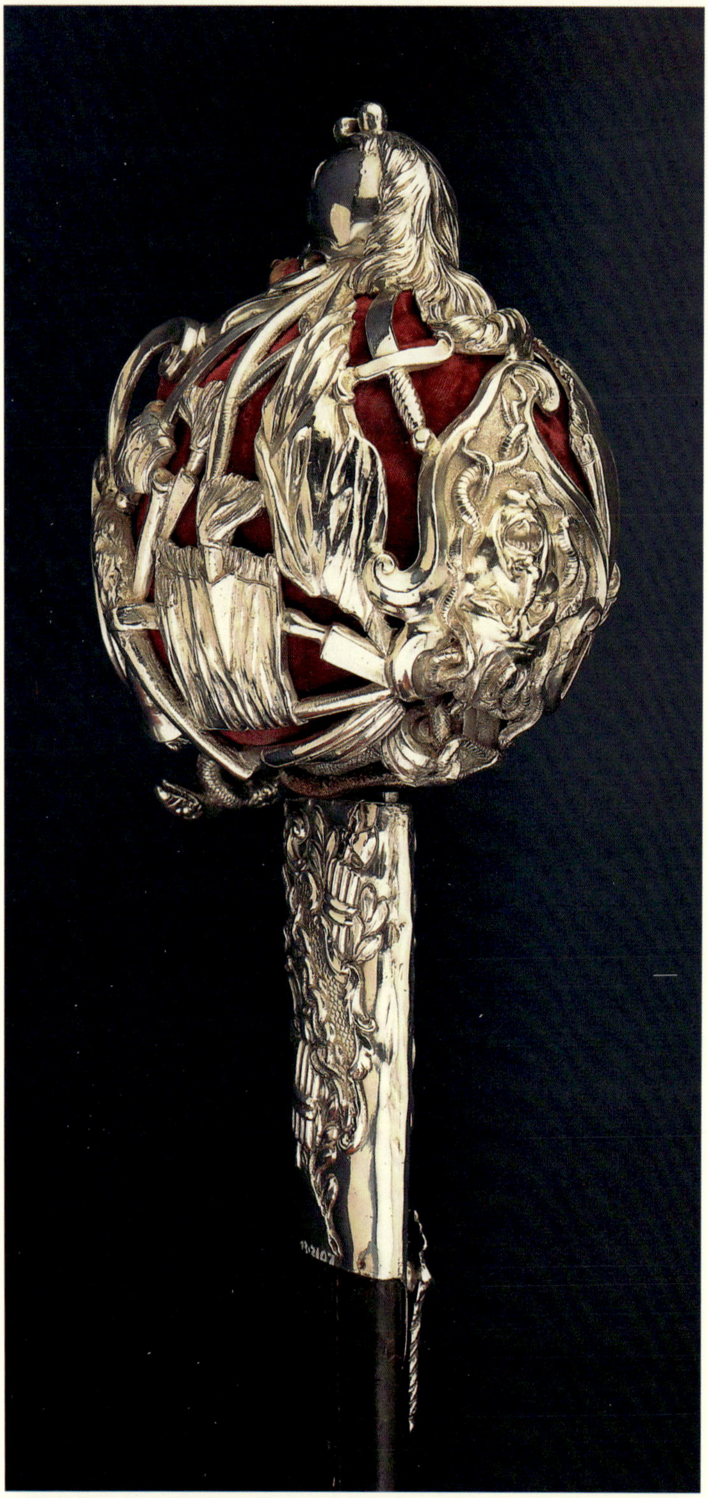

Drambuie Ltd

PRINCE CHARLES EDWARD STUART: ENGRAVING BY ROBERT STRANGE. NOTE THE MOTIFS IN THE BOTTOM RIGHT-HAND CORNER: CROSS-HILTED SWORD, TARGE WITH MEDUSA HEAD AND CLASSICAL HELMET.

1:49 Basket-hilted backsword (claidheamh cùil)

Hilt, probably north European, second quarter 18th century; blade, probably German, and contemporary with the hilt.

Hilt of unmarked silver. The pommel has a dolphin's head on its brow, facing to the rear. The basket, which is of conventional shape, but outlined with rococo scrolls, is constructed of numerous small pieces cast in low relief and soldered together. There are no forward-guards. The decoration consists of two military trophies, classical and modern, and between them, in front of the fingers, a vigorous head of Medusa. The quillons are in the form of two entwined serpents, their heads forming the wrist-guard.

The grip is covered with white rayskin and spirally bound at intervals with twists of silver wire. Turk's-head ferrules. The buff-leather liner is covered with crimson velvet.

The straight, one-edged blade has a ricasso 1" long, two narrow contiguous fullers, and a false edge 9" long.

The scabbard is of black leather with two silver mounts, the top one with a belt-hook near its lower edge cast as a cornucopia. The mouthpiece is embossed on each face with a fasces, a shield charged with a Medusa's head, and a laurel branch. The crampet, which has a small symmetrical trail, is embossed with a fasces, a quiver, and the Union flowers.

Length overall, $38\frac{9}{16}$".

This sword came to Brodie through the marriage of Elizabeth Brodie (1794-1864) to George, 5th Duke of Gordon(1770-1836), with the tradition that it had been taken from the Prince's baggage train after Culloden. The silver mounted targe from the great hall of Warwick has matching decorative features.

Lender: The National Trust for Scotland (Brodie Castle).

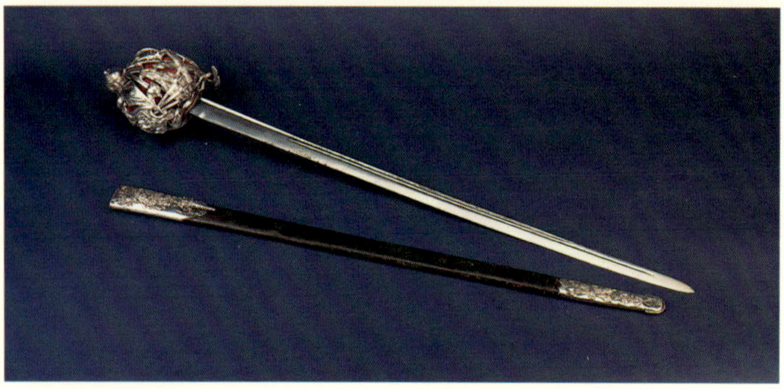

1:50 Basket-hilted sword (claidheamh mòr)

Hilt, probably north-European, second quarter 18th century; blade, European, probably early 17th century.

Hilt of chiselled and pierced iron, partially russeted and partially fire-gilt. The pommel is writhen. The basket, which is outlined with rococo scrolls, is decorated on each face with a trophy, the outer one representing the liberal arts, and the inner one war. Between them is a lion sejant supporting a shield of arms; paly of ten. The wrist-guard, which is $4^{5}/_{16}$" long, is chiselled with leaves. Riveted into the openings flanking the rear quillon are two small plaques each chiselled in relief with a rococo shield. That on the outer side bears the arms of France (modern) and the other those of England. Engraved on the scrolls near the pommel is AMOR OMNIBUS IDEM.

The barrel-shaped grip is covered with black leather and bound with a herring-bone of silver wire. The pasteboard liner is covered with crimson velvet.

The straight, two-edged blade, which is of flattened-hexagonal section, has a narrow fuller. Stamped in the fuller on the outer face is DOMINE, and on the inner face MAESTRE, each word between a pair of so-called 'sickle marks'. Incised on the flat is a passion cross on a recercely base.

Length overall, $40^{11}/_{16}$".

The arms probably represent those of Atholl; paly of six, or and sable. This is traditionally the sword of William Murray, Marquis of Tullibardine, the attained Duke of Atholl. His dukedom had been conferred on his younger brother, James, a supporter of the House of Hanover. The Marquis accompanied the Prince from France and, despite poor health, served throughout the campaign. He surrendered himself a few days after Culloden to William Buchanan the younger of Drumakill, and died a prisoner in July of the same year.

'It was about seven o'clock in the morning that Buchanan was told that some travellers were at his gate seeking for a guide. Going out to them, he found Tullibardine, Vezzosi, and four servants, mounted on wretched horses, "att the head of the avenue in a very distress'd condition," and after a brief conversation realised who and what they were. The Marquis it seems had a view to surrendering to General Campbell, "but as he was not available soon agreed to Buchanan's suggestion that he should come into Drumakill house, and gave up his sword, telling Buchanan shortly afterwards to keep it as a present".'[1]

Lender: Geoffrey Jenkinson.

1 Fergusson, p 184.

William Murray, Marquis of Tullibardine, by an unknown artist (c1720).

1:51 *Basket-hilted cavalry backsword*

Hilt, British, probably about 1740-55; blade, probably German.

The iron hilt consists of a bun pommel with a rather tall cylindrical tang-button, and a basket of more or less conventional Highland type, except that it lacks the additional rear-guards, and the saltire bars on the forward corner of each shield towards the pommel combine to form a rounded arch. The rear quillon does not project beyond the perimeter of the basket. The bars, which are of flattened-rectangular section, are plain and unpierced.

The grip is covered in black rayskin, but the wire binding is missing, as are the original buff-leather liner and sword-knot.

The plain, straight, one-edged blade has two narrow, contiguous fullers, and a false edge approximately 6 1/2" long.

Length overall, 39 3/4".

Swords of this type were purchased by the colonels of British cavalry regiments, both horse and dragoons, for the use of their men. Comparable weapons are illustrated in the paintings of British heavy cavalry by David Morier, 1751, at Windsor Castle.[1]

Lender: Edinburgh Castle (on loan from the Royal Armouries).

1 Miller & Dawnay, Cat Nos 70-72, 74-76, 80-82, 84-9,-113.

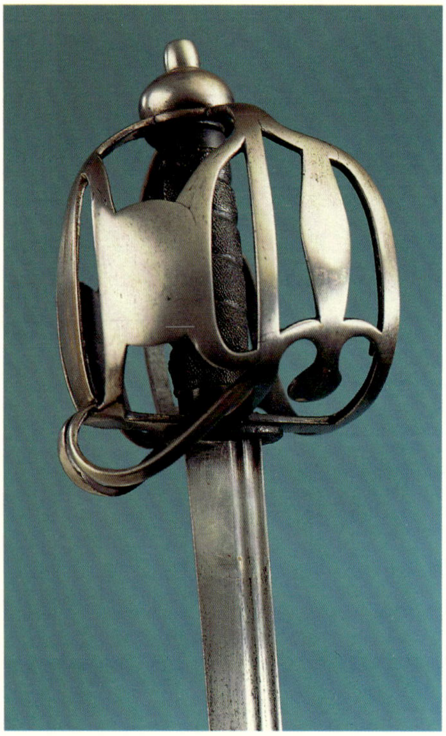

1:52 *British cavalry sword*

Hilt, British, first half 18th century; blade, possiby German.

The brass hilt consists of a pommel with a flattened tang-button, and guards consisting of a knuckle-guard, its end plugged into the pommel, a short comma-shaped rear quillon supporting at their junction a pair of oval shells, one on each face, the forward edge of each linked to the knuckle-guard by a short strut.

The grip is bound with twists of brass of various gauges, some plain and some twisted.

The plain, straight, two-edged, hollow-ground blade is of diamond section.

Length overall, 41 1/8". A somewhat comparable hilt is illustrated in the portrait of Lieutenant James Dalrymple, 2nd Dragoons, painted about 1751, at Prestonfield House, Midlothian.

Lender: Scottish United Services Museum, Edinburgh (Acq No M1995-28)

1:53 *Basket-hilted cavalry backsword*

Hilt, British, probably about 1740-55; blade, probably German.

The iron hilt consists of a bun pommel and a basket of more or less conventional Highland type, except that the saltire bars on the forward corner of each shield towards the pommel combine to form a rounded arch. The rear quillon does not project beyond the perimeter of the basket. The bars are of rounded section. The edges of the broad guards are cut with broad shallow scallops alternating with fishtail merlons and the edges of the shields with pairs of similar scallops with a broad concave-ended merlon at the centre. The piercing includes hearts of conventional shape.

The grip is covered in black rayskin bound with coarse wire. The original buff-leather liner and sword-knot are missing.

The plain, straight, one-edged blade has a shoulder 1/8" long, and a narrow fuller close to the spine 26 1/2" long. All now somewhat corroded.

Length overall, 42 5/16".

Lender: Scottish United Services Museum, Edinburgh. (Acq No A1905-216).

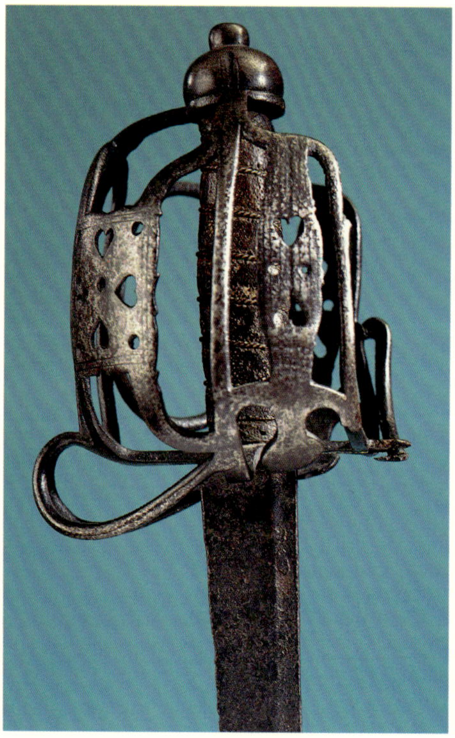

1:54 *British infantry hanger*

British, second quarter 18th century.

Hilt of iron, the pommel now missing. The guards include a knuckle-guard, the end of which would originally have been plugged into the pommel, and a short comma-shaped rear quillon. At their junction these support a pair of oval shells, one on each face, the forward edge of each linked to the knuckle-guard by a short scroll-guard. On the outside of the hand the rim of the shell is linked to the end of the grip by a broad, drop-shaped plate pierced by two D-shaped openings back to back.

The turned wooden grip is modern.

The plain, curved, one-edged blade has a narrow fuller and a false edge. The point is worn away. Stamped on each face in bold Roman capitals is HERVE.

Length overall, 32".

Hangers with hilts of this type are illustrated by Bernard Lens in *The Grenadiers' Exercise of the Grenade in His Majesty's First Regt of Footguards. Designed for the use of His Royal Highness the Duke of Cumberland*, 1735.

Although the inscription is struck very heavily on each face there is no sign whatever of a terminal letter Y. The blade is not, therefore, the product of the well-known Harvey workshop in Birmingham.

Lender: Scottish United Services Museum, Edinburgh (Acq No M1935-61).

1:55 *Silver-hilted small-sword* (claidheamh cùil)

Hilt, English about 1735; blade probably German.

The hilt consists of a pommel, a guard before the hand shaped like a symmetrical figure-of-eight, and a sleeve supporting a knuckle-guard, its end plugged into the front of the pommel, a rear quillon, and a pair of slender arms of the hilt. Cast and chased in low relief with foliate *Régence* decoration sometimes ending in the heads of grotesque beasts. Struck on the inner face of the knuckle-guard are three marks, now almost illegible. One is a maker's mark of two letters, another is almost certainly the lower edge of the English standard mark.

The grip is spirally bound with a foil alternating with a herring-bone of coarse wire all in silver.

The straight three-edged blade is hollow-ground.

Length overall, 37$^{7}/_{8}$".

This type of sword, although the descendant of a fighting rapier, was worn in the 18th century as a sign of gentility, and in this case as a form of costume jewellery. The decoration of small-sword hilts changed with every wind of fashion.

Possibly the dress sword of Alexander Irvine of Drum, the 17th laird, who joined Prince Charles at Edinburgh, was present at Culloden and, escaping after the defeat, was for a time concealed at Drum Castle. He was excepted from pardon in the Act of Indemnity, but escaped forfeiture by the grand jury, who twice threw out bills for treason and returned an 'ignoramus' verdict at Edinburgh in October 1748. Alexander died at his seat of Drum in 1761. See also 1:57, 7:8, 10:10.

Lender: The National Trust for Scotland (Drum Castle).

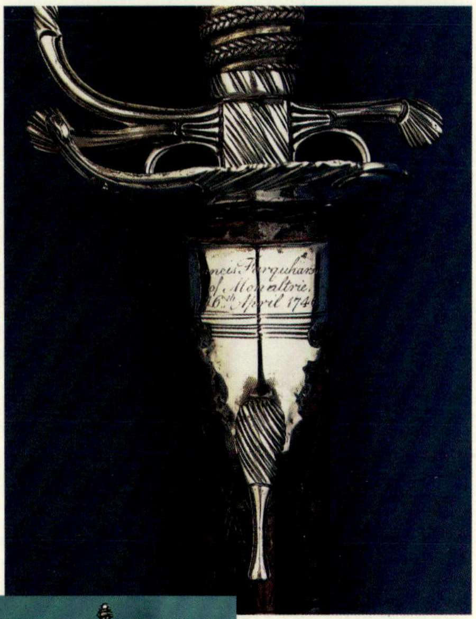

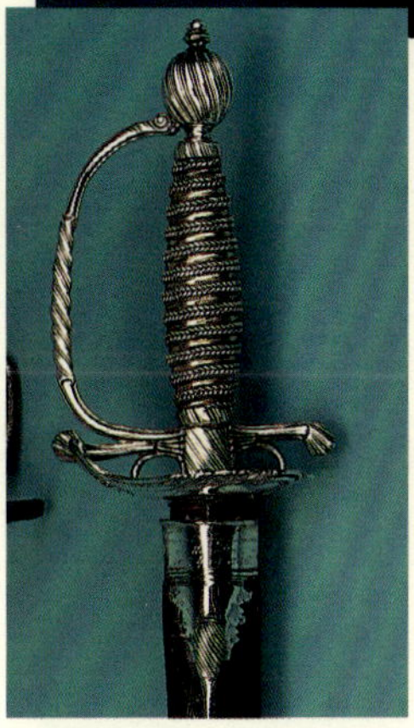

1:56 *Silver-hilted small sword* (claidheamh cùil)

Hilt, English (London) 1759-60; blade, probably German.

The hilt is similar in form to that of 1:52, except that the sleeve is shorter, the arms of the hilt are smaller, and the guard before the hand is shaped like a heart, its lobes to the rear, and its point divided to accommodate the forward quillon. Cast and chased with writhen decoration. Struck on the inner face of the knuckle-guard are four marks; 1) the maker's mark W K in a shaped punch; 2) the lion passant, the standard mark; 3) the crowned leopard's head of London; and 4) the Gothic D, the date-letter for 1759/60. The first two marks are also stuck on the shell towards the hand. Engraved on the shell towards the blade is 'Francis Farquharson of Monaltrie 16th April 1746'.

The straight, three-edged blade, which is hollow-ground, narrows sharply about 8$^{1}/_{2}$" from the hilt.

The scabbard, which is of brown leather, blind-tooled, has two silver mounts, the top one with a belt-hook. Engraved on the front of the locket is the same inscription as on the hilt.

Length overall, 40$^{1}/_{8}$".

The blade is shaped in this way so that a considerable parrying movement can be achieved by a relatively slight motion of the wrist.

The maker's mark is that of William Kinman, probably the best known London hilt-maker of his day. His first recorded mark was entered at Goldsmiths' Hall on 31 January 1759. A second mark was entered by him, or perhaps a son, on 17 May 1782.[1]

Known as Baron Ban because of his fine bearing (from the Gaelic *bàn*, meaning handsome), Francis Farquharson of Monaltrie was captured after Culloden, sent to the Tower of London, sentenced to death, reprieved on the day of his execution and spent the next 16 years in captivity.

1 Grimwade, p 572, mark no 3210.

Lender: Capt Alwyne Compton Farquharson of Invercauld.

Right: Alexander Irvine of Drum, by Cosmo Alexander (c1740).

Far right: Francis Farquharson of Monaltrie, by an unknown artist (c1760).

1:58 *Silver-hilted hanger or cutto*

Hilt, English, second quarter 18th century; blade, German (Solingen), 17th-century.

The hilt of stained horn spirally-fluted or writhen (with silver tang-button), tapers towards the blade. A pair of short recurved quillons, their ends decorated with cast petals, support at their centre a chased silver shell-guard outside the hand turned towards the blade.

The straight, one-edged blade, has two broad fullers. Signed HEINRICH KOLL ME FECIT. The blade is a cut-down backsword blade of the 17th century.

Length 26½".

The black leather scabbard has two suspension rings, top and middle locket and chape all of silver. The top locket has a cast silver belt-hook.

The silver hilt bears a maker's mark I B (see below). The sword has not been removed from its case and no examination of the other silver marks has been made. Thanks are due to Claude Blair for his detailed information on this sword.

Possibly the work of John Bennett II, Citizen and Barber Surgeon of London, apprenticed 14 April 1747. In 1773 he is recorded as a hilt maker on Threadneedle Street.[1]

This is known to be the sword of General James Wolfe, the victor of Quebec, who fought at Culloden as a young man.

Lender: John St A Warde, Squerreys Court.

1 Grimwade, p 433.

ABOVE: CAPTAIN (LATER GENERAL) JAMES WOLFE, BY AN UNKNOWN ARTIST (C1740)

1:57 *Silver-hilted hunting sword (hanger or cutto)*

Hilt, London 1733/4; blade probably German.

The hilt consists of a solid grip tapering evenly towards the blade, a shallow sleeve supporting both a rear quillon and a knuckle-guard, its end plugged into the front of the grip at the further end, and a separate shell-guard outside the hand turned towards the blade. Cast and chiselled, partly against a matted ground, with scenes from classical mythology. Struck on the inner face of the knuckle-guards are four marks; 1) the maker's mark WS; 2) the English standard mark; 3) the London assay mark; and 4) the London date-letter S for 1733/4.

The straight, one-edged blade has two narrow fullers, and a false edge.

Length overall, 26⅝".

The maker's mark is probably that of William Strange, who was free of the Cutlers' Company, by service to John Carman, on 13 October 1724. He entered his mark at Goldsmiths' Hall, London, on 9 June, 1725, giving his address as New Street Square. By 1743 he was insolvent.[1]

This type of a short sword was worn not only for hunting, but also when travelling or out at night.

Possibly the sword of Alexander Irvine of Drum, the 17th Laird, who was out in '45. See 1:55, 7:8, 10:10.

Lender: The National Trust for Scotland (Drum Castle).

1 Grimwade, No 3298, p 673.

1:59 *Sword blade from the fence at Twickenham House*

Many captured Scottish sword blades were used after Culloden to act as low iron fences. 30" long.

Lender: The Duke of Argyll.

DAGGERS AND DIRKS

2:1 *Silver-mounted quillon dagger (whinger)*

Lowland Scottish (possibly Kilmaurs), dated 1729.

The haft consists of a pair of short, straight quillons, each ending in a knob, and a grip covered with tortoiseshell, tapering evenly towards the blade and with a domed cap and a ferrule edged with stylised acanthus tips.

The straight, one-edged blade is of isosceles section for 4$^{1}/_{8}$" and thereafter of a variety of triangular sections, due to the spine being filed to an irregular wavy shape. The first section of the spine is engraved 1 7 2 9, with a small round hole pierced after each figure. The second section is crudely filed and engraved with the very stylised heads and necks of two grotesque beasts. Thereafter there are crudely made stars in pairs or singly in each dip of the waves. A series of four round holes is pierced through the blade near its spine, starting at the haft. Each is connected to one of the holes in the spine.

The sheath, which is of brown leather, blind-tooled, has three mounts (the crampet missing), the middle locket with holes for two implements, and the lowest one with a hole for a single one (all are missing). The leather on the reverse is pierced by two thongs for suspension.

Length overall, 18$^{25}/_{32}$".

The catalogue of the Armoury of George IV records that 2:1 was received in March 1822 from the collection of George III (No 3156). It may be the 'Short hanger tortoiseshell gripe Silver mo[u]nted with two knives and a fork' listed in the post-mortem inventory of the Duke of Cumberland.[1] The Duke's collection passed to George III.

A very similar dagger in the Museum of Antiquities, Edinburgh, complete with its byeknife and fork, bears a mark on its blade very similar to that on the blade of a hanger which is in addition marked KILMARES on both hilt and blade.[2] This is thought to stand for Kilmaurs, a small burgh in Ayrshire, formerly well-known for the cutlery produced there.[3]

Lent by Her Majesty The Queen.

1 Cumberland Papers, Vol I, p 61.

2 Reg No LC 53; Wallace, Pls 74-5 and Pl 78, repectively.

3 Reid, in *Connoisseur*.

I am most grateful to Philip Lankester for his help in cataloguing this dagger.

Literature: Laking, *Armoury of Windsor Castle*, No 9; Laking, *European Arms and Armour*, III, fig 816.

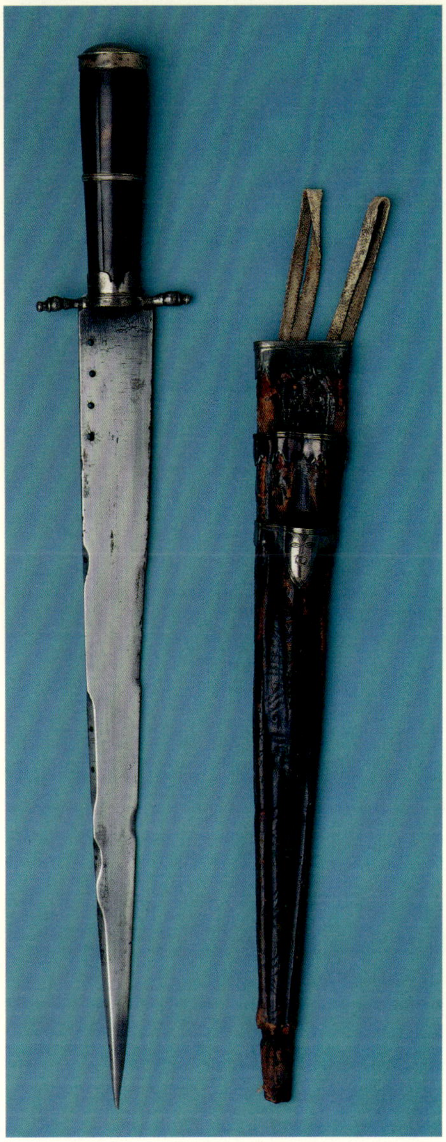

2.2 *Dirk (biodag)*

Highland, mid-18th century. Haft of dark, closely-grained wood. The large, flat pommel, which has a circular cap of brass pierced with a running scroll, is decorated on the underside with two rows of small punched circles; the narrow grip, which swells slightly from pommel to haunches, is carved with vigorous knotwork in high relief consisting of two adjacent bands of four-ply plait, the interspaces filled with knobs; the haunches are narrow, deep, and parallel-sided, the carving finer than that of the grip from which it is quite disconnected. The interlace on each face consists of three triangular knots. The rear haunch is thicker than its pair and its edge is decorated with a lightly incised scroll and small punched circles. The brass mount on the lower edge of the haft is convex towards the blade.

The plain, straight, one-edged blade, which tapers fairly evenly from haft to point, is taken from a backsword. It has two narrow fullers near the spine, the rear one obliterated by the cutting of the false edge after 2$^{1}/_{2}$" and the second one after 5$^{3}/_{4}$".

Length overall, 20$^{15}/_{16}$".

Very many early dirks have blades made out of old sword blades. The scabbard of this dirk survives, but is too fragile for exhibition. It probably dates, like the byeknife and fork in its pockets, from after the 1782 repeal of the Act against the wearing of Highland dress.

A very similar dirk is illustrated in the portrait of John Campbell, 4th Earl of Loudon, in the uniform of his Regiment, painted by Allan Ramsay in 1747.[1]

Lender: Scottish United Services Museum (Acq No M1932-187).

1 Property of the Marquess of Bute.

Literature: Anderson & Drummond, Pl XIX, No 11; C E Whitelaw, *Captain N R Colville*. Norman, in *Journal of Arms and Armour Society*, pp 6-9, Pl I B.

2:3 Dirk (biodag)

*c*1700-25. Hilt of solid cast brass. The grip is moulded in high relief and engraved on the haunches and on the underside of the pommel. The iron tang nut is ornamentally notched.

The blade is single-edged with one fuller down the back and on each face. It is secured by a tang nut.

The sheath has two side pockets but the fittings are missing. It would appear never to have had metal mounts. The leather is tooled on the back of the sheath and above the top pocket, which is also stamped A+L 1744.

Length overall, $18\frac{3}{4}$".

Lender: Glasgow Museums (1940-45 cy: CEW 895).

2:4 Dirk (biodag)

Mid-18th century. The hilt is of bog oak carved with interlace work and the underside of the pommel fluted. The surviving mounts consist of a brass pommel cap (the haunch mounts missing).

The narrow blade bears two fullers and would appear to be a cut-down sword blade. It is secured by a tang nut.

The sheath, along with its fittings, is missing.

Length overall, $20\frac{11}{16}$".

Lender: Glasgow Museums (1939-65ng).

Literature: Scott, Vol II, Section IV.

2:5 Dirk (biodag)

*c*1744. Hilt of bog oak carved with interlace work in low relief and the underside of the pommel fluted. The mounts are of brass, the pommel cap with a bead on edge and incised lines on top. The side straps of haunch mount are missing. The tang nut is in the form of a moulded knob.

The blade has one curved fuller on each face and is notched and incised with lines and dots on the back. The tang is burred over a large button.

The leather sheath has two side pockets, the mount of one pierced with a heart-shaped perforation and incised with lines. The mount of the other and the knife and fork are missing. The upper mount bears the incised initials H*McL, obviously the initials of the owner. The dirk was suspended by the leather loop sewn at the back below the brass locket.

Length overall, $17\frac{3}{8}$".

Lender: Glasgow Museums (1940-45 ch: CEW 103).

2:6 Brass-mounted Highland dirk

The haft consists of a brass ferrule with shallow crescent where it meets the blade and incised line between blade and grip. The grip is of dark hardwood finely carved in Celtic interlace and with round-shouldered haunches forming the guard. The circular brass pommel is decorated with vertical lines around the circumference, with the top of open-work, showing replacement red material.

The straight one-edge blade is notched for three-quarters of its length. The threaded tang is secured to the hasp by a decorative star-shaped nut.

Length overall, 14".

This dirk was found with other objects in 1905 at Kings Stables on Culloden Moor.

Lender: Museum of Antiquities, Edinburgh.

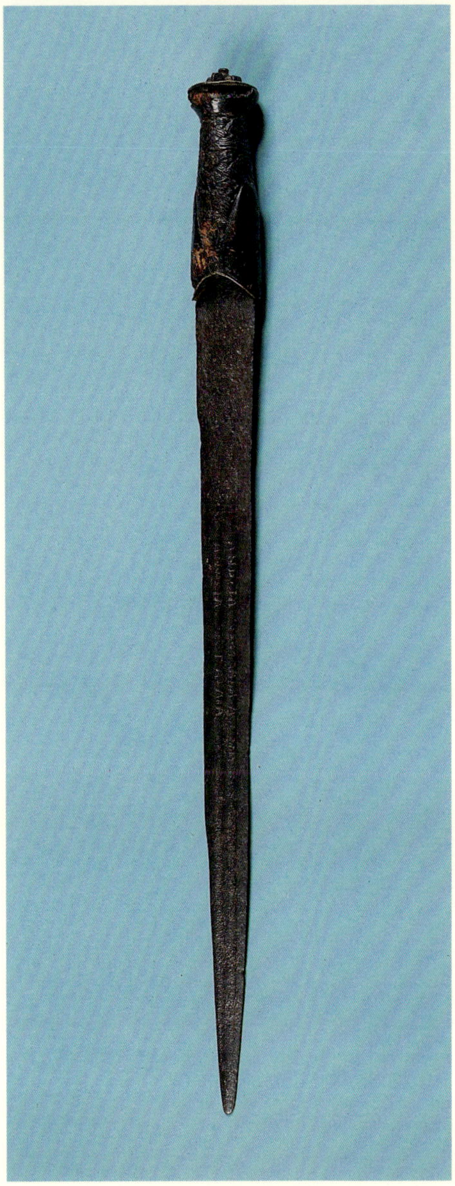

2:7 Brass-mounted Highland dirk

The haft comprises a shallow crescent of brass where the grip meets the blade. The hardwood grip is carved with Celtic interlace with two long lobes forming the guard. Pommel of undecorated brass.

The two-edged blade from a claymore, with *Andrea Farara* engraved in the fullers. The threaded tang is secured to the haft by a star-shaped nut. *c*1700.

Length overall, 19".

From the collection of Lord Lovat.

Lender: Mrs Ann Gloag (Beaufort Castle).

2:8 Knife (sgian)

Probably Scottish, 18th century.

The cylindrical haft is of ivory with a brass pommel-cap and ferrule.

The one-edged blade has a clipped point (now slightly broken). Stamped on one face is a mark consisting of part of the edge of a cog-wheel and the letters PAU.

The black leather sheath, which has a brass crampet, is presumably of later date.

Length overall, 8 1/4".

It is said that this knife was taken from the side of a horse on the field of Culloden. Known as the White Knife of Dal Moraisd.

Lender: The Duke of Atholl.

Lochaber Axes

By Jackie Moran

In the early 16th century a long shafted weapon was developed in Scotland called the Lochaber axe. It was still in use two centuries later but it cannot be said with certainty whether a 16th-century Lochaber axe bore any resemblance to what we recognise as an 18th-century one. The later axes had a long blade with a hook projecting backwards from the tip of the shaft.

Lochaber axes were carried by town guards in burghs such as Aberdeen and Edinburgh. The town guards of Edinburgh are known to have been armed with them by the time of the Porteous Riot of 1736.

At Culloden many of the Highlanders carried them and there were many home-made staff weapons consisting of scythe blades mounted on long shafts producing lethal weapons. The Lochaber axe was by far the most commonly used.

3:2 Scottish Lochaber axe

The blade, with detached hook, fitted into shaft top. Similar to the axes that were used by the Town Guard of Aberdeen. *c*1700. 76" long.

Lender: William Keith Neal Foundation.

3:1 Scottish Lochaber axe

The blade with a projecting knife forming part of the main blade. *c*1700. 100" long.

Lender: The Duke of Argyll (Inveraray Castle).

Literature: Caldwell, 'Some notes on Scottish axes and long-shafted weapons', in Caldwell, pp 288-90 and 29-305.

Highland Targes

By Jackie Moran

LORD GEORGE MURRAY, BY AN UNKNOWN ARTIST (C1740).

The word 'targe' has no real meaning for us until the 17th century, when it signifies the shield carried by the Highland fighting man. Targes are circular, around 20" in diameter and are normally very strongly constructed of oak or pine, or a combination of both. Two layers of wood are laid across each other for strength and covered with cow hide. The surface of the leather has designs tooled on it in panels of varying shapes which may be outlined and emphasised by brass- or silver-headed studs of different sizes. There is almost always a central boss of brass which may be pierced to take a spike. On some targes the boss is lined with cow-horn and forms a drinking cup.

The backing is most commonly cow, calf, goat or deerskin with the fur outwards. In order to absorb shock, stuffing was often packed under the backing leather. Any convenient material seems to have been used, for example scraps of calf or deerskin, loose animal hair or straw. The back of the targe also has a leather arm-strap or loop, a hand-grip and straps by which it was slung on the back when not in use. If fitted with a spike, a scabbard is provided on the back to keep the spike. This a very rare feature and found on only one recorded extant targe.

The earliest dated targe is in the Hunterian Museum, Glasgow. The date 1623 is engraved on its brass boss. There are eight, possibly nine, other targes dated between 1708 and 1723 and one as late as 1755. Dating on stylistic grounds is not easy. As with powder horns the quality of the decoration, particularly the interlace, is a good guide, with the best being the earliest. Charles E Whitelaw, who did much for the study and preservation of Highland weapons, distinguished three types of decoration on the surface of the targe.

TYPE A is divided by circles of studs laid off from the centre of the targe, forming bands. These bands may be subdivided into compartments and are tooled with Celtic interlace ornament, running leaf scrolls or grotesque animals.

TYPE B is occupied by one central and four or six surrounding panels which are circular or diamond in shape and outlined by brass studs with a brass boss in the centre of each. The surface of the leather is tooled with Celtic interlace ornament or leaf scrolls.

TYPE C is divided by lines of studs radiating from the centre of the targe, forming a star. The exposed surface of the leather is again tooled with Celtic interlace ornament or leaf scrolls.

From the 1640s to the 1740s Highlanders used the new combination of broadswords and targes to win many victories over their enemies. They would run unencumbered by heavy guns or other equipment at the enemy's line and at close quarters the combination of the targe and slashing sword proved far more versatile than the pikes and muskets of their adversaries. This tactic in warfare is now known as The Highland Charge.

Culloden appears to have been the last occasion this tactic was used in a major pitched battle. There is a story that many of the Highlanders discarded their targes for the intended night attack on Cumberland's army before the battle, and were less effective on the field.

James, 3rd Duke of Perth, after Allan Ramsay.

SNPG

4:1 Silver mounted targe decorated with trophies in cast silver

Brown pigskin with shallow embossed detail entirely decorated with cast-silver trophies, the central boss taking the form of the head of Medusa, the mouth threaded to take a spike. The back is covered with deer skin. The arm-strap and hand-grip are missing. Some silver nails were replaced in 1986. 1740. 18⁹/₁₀" diam.

Believed to have been commissioned by James, 3rd Duke of Perth. Two full sets of Highland dress were made as gifts, one to Prince Charles, the other to his brother Henry. The silver mounts applied to the targe both feature the head of Medusa in the centre, reflecting the silver-hilted sword from Brodie Castle (No 1:49). Close comparison of the hilt shows similarities of decoration to that on the targe. An engraving of the Young Pretender by Sir Robert Strange shows a helmet, sword, and targe with Medusa head; the helmet is of the same type as the pommel of the Brodie sword. That this targe and sword match each other in many features is without doubt. Credit is due to A V B Norman for this suggestion.

A similar targe is in the collection of the Museum of Antiquities, Edinburgh. It has less silver nail decoration.

Lender: Warwick Castle

4:2 Scottish Highland targe

Carried at Culloden by Small of Dirnanean. Covered with cowhide decorated with brass nails, the boss engraved with the date 1707. The back covered in deerskin. *c*1700. 20" diam.

Lender: The Duke of Atholl (Blair Castle).

4:4 Scottish Highland targe

Covered in dark cowhide decorated with raised interlaced ornament, the centre with HONOR THE KING FEAR GOD. One large and two smaller holes, believed to be bullet holes. The back is covered in deerskin. *c*1730. 24" diam.

Lender: Sir Donald Cameron of Lochiel.

Detail of Prince Charles Edward Stuart's fowling piece (No 5:4) showing the thistle surmounted by royal crown, as in the targe illustrated below (No 4:3).

4:3 Scottish Highland targe

Decorated with brass studs and nails arranged to form four crowns surmounting stylised thistles, the cowhide with feint embossed floral decoration. The back with torn deerskin, and old label, signed by the committee, the History and Historical Arts Exhibition. *c*1700. 19" diam.

Lender: Geoffrey Jenkinson (ex William Keith Neal).

4:5 *Scottish Highland targe*

Covered in embossed cowhide decorated with brass studs and nails. Triangular pierced brass pieces adorn the front and are used on the deerskin back to reinforce the arm-strap and hand-grip. Used by a Grant of Glenmoriston in the 1719 Rising. *c*1700. 20" diam.

Lender: Ian Grant of Glenmoriston.

4:6 *Scottish Highland targe*

Cowhide decorated with interlaced foliate and traditional scrolls, brass triangular pierced plates and large brass domes. *c*1745. 19" diam.

Lender: Duke of Argyll (Inveraray Castle).

4:7 *Scottish Highland targe*

Covered in dark cowhide decorated with engraved brass studs, formed into concentric circles. Embossed leather decorated to the highest quality in the true Highland manner. The reverse covered in deerskin with original arm-strap and hand-grip, with a label saying Moy Hall. *c*1700. 19" diam.

Lender: William Keith Neal Foundation.

4:8 *Scottish Highland targe*

Similar to 4:7 but with lesser quality embossed leather decoration. The reverse with small fragment of cowhide, and missing its arm-strap and hand-grip. *c*1730. 19" diam.

Lender: The National Trust for Scotland (Culloden).

4:9 *Scottish Highland targe*

Decorated with a series of brass bosses over tooled cowhide. The large engraved brass central boss has a threaded metal spike which screws into the centre of the boss. The back of the targe is covered in deerskin; the arm-strap is missing, a leather scabbard for the spike and the hand-grip survive. *c*1740. 19" diam.

This is the only recorded targe known to have its original iron spike.

Lender: Private collection.

4:11 *Scottish Highland targe*

Covered in dark leather decorated with small brass-headed nails, interlaced on the outer edge and wavy tooling in relief towards the centre. The back is covered in deerskin. Both arm-strap and hand-grip are missing. It bears an owner's wax seal. *c*1720. 21" diam.

Lender: The National Trust For Scotland (Craigievar Castle).

4:10 *Scottish Highland targe*

Covered on the front with dark cowhide decorated with nine panels of Celtic inversed interlace design. The panels framed in brass-headed nails of varying sizes, many of them missing. The cowhide is torn in places. The central brass boss is reeded with a central plain brass button. The back is covered in deerskin and complete with adjustable arm-strap and hand-grip. *c*1700. 19" diam.

Traditionally known as the Cromarty Targe.

Lender: Private collection.

4:12 *Scottish Highland targe*

Covered in dark cowhide, decorated with raised interlace and with brass-headed nails. The central boss engraved with the initials AG & DG and 166?, with a crude engraved yew tree, the badge of Lord Lovat. The back is missing its cover, arm-strap and hand-grip. *c*1669. 19" diam.

Traditionally known as Lord Lovat's targe.

Lender: Mrs Ann Gloag (Beaufort Castle).

Some notes on firearms and their collectors

By John Batty

Shooting with firearms was so popular in Scotland in the sixteenth century that various proclamations were issued banning their use. It is therefore surprising that so very few Scottish long guns survive. The largest group, comprising seventeen pieces, is in the Museum of Antiquities, Edinburgh. This is a small number when compared with Continental guns of the same period. One only has to look at the weapon collections in Austria and Germany to wonder what has become of our Scottish guns.

Not only was the Highland way of life lost after the defeat at Culloden, but a substantial number of long guns must have been lost also. We know that many imported weapons were used by the Jacobite army but there must also have been many indigenous weapons in use. Scottish firearms have a distinctive design which is more suggestive of the Middle East than of Europe, with pistol stocks made entirely of steel, brass, or a combination of both. Often with high quality silver inlay, they are now highly prized by collectors.

Drambuie Ltd

A HIGHLAND SOLDIER IN THE SERVICE OF KING GEORGE II: NOTE THE INITIALS 'GR' ON THE AMMUNITION POUCH.

The butts are of a variety of shapes, and form fish-tails, lemons, hearts and scrolls. Many combine a butt finial, known as a pricker, with a sharp thin spike which unscrews and can be used to clear the touch-hole of burned powder. Many seventeenth-century pistols are engraved with fine floral decoration, and some are dated, usually at the breech and the fence (the disc on the side of the powder pan).

Some of the very earliest Scottish pistols had wooden stocks but few have survived. The early gun and rifle stocks are also of unconventional design and, like the pistols, could be mistaken for the work of Middle-Eastern craftsmen. Paddle-shaped butts combined with large snaphaunce locks and workmanship of high quality set them apart from other long guns.

Long guns or muskets used in warfare by the Scots are described by Marshal Wade in his 1724 report to his superiors on the Highlanders' method of attack:

'The Arms they make use of in War, are, a Musket, a Broad Sword and Target, a Pistol and Dirk or Dagger, hanging by their side, with Powder Horn and Pouch for their Ammunition. They form themselves into Bodies of unequal numbers according to the strength of their Clan or Tribe, which is commanded by their Respective Superior or Chieftain. When in sight of the enemy they possess themselves of the highest Ground, believing they descend on them with greater force. They generally give their fire at a distance, then lay down their Arms on the ground and make a vigorous attack with their Broad Swords.'

When the collection of the Grants of Freuchie was sold in 1977 it contained 13 long guns whose survival was perhaps due rather to the Lairds of Grant's loyalty to the House of Hanover than to the Jacobite cause.

All Highlanders were ordered to surrender their weapons to the government army after the 1719 Rebellion when the government Disarming Act of 1725 was introduced, and again in 1746 after the defeat at Culloden. Long guns would have been harder to conceal than pistols, therefore more pistols survive than guns. Reports show that many of the weapons handed in were of poor quality: the best no doubt would have been concealed. It is not beyond the bounds of possibility that swords were dismantled, blades hidden, and hilts displayed as ornaments, particularly the fine cast silver guards.

Wearing of Highland dress was forbidden and it mattered not if the family had been loyal to the Crown. This caused much resentment and made life hard for the Highlander who had depended on his long plaid for warmth and protection from the harsh elements when tending stock on the hill.

Some Highlanders were ordered to swear on oath:

'I do swear, and as I shall have to answer to God at the Great Day of Judgement, I have not nor shall have in my possession, any gun, sword, pistol or arm whatsoever; and never use any tartan, plaid or any part of the Highland garb; and if I do so, may I be cursed in my undertakings, family, and property – may I never see my wife and children, father, mother and relations – may I be killed in battle as a coward and lie without Christian burial, in a strange land, far from the graves of my forefathers and kindred; may all this come across me if I break my oath.'

A fine flintlock turnabout or Wender sporting gun by Bourdiec, Paris, was given by Prince Charles Edward Stuart to David, Lord Elcho. It was subsequently bequeathed to Donald Cameron of Lochiel. The top barrel carries a Jacobite motto with a thistle surmounted by a royal crown inlaid in gold at the breech. It was possibly made for the Old Pretender, the exiled King James VIII, c1730. It had two barrels, one above the other: to fire it, both barrels would be primed with a measured amount of black powder from a powder flask. Then wadding would be rammed down, followed by a measure of shot, then more wadding. The pan would usually be primed with finer powder than the breech and the touch-hole cleared of any residual burnt powder from the previous shot.

Detail of a flintlock service pistol, dated 1742

The flint, which was held tightly between the jaws of the cock, would be checked to ensure it was in good condition. Leather wrapped around the flint assured a firm fit, and avoided any damage when the top jaw screw was tightened. The flint would be lined up so it struck the steel at the perfect angle for ignition. When the trigger was squeezed, the flint in the jaws of the cock sprang forward at high speed, scraping minute particles of burning steel into the pan full of gunpowder. This explosion forced ignition through the touch-hole, setting off the main charge in the breech. This caused the shot to leave the muzzle at great velocity and, with good aiming, it would hit the target.

Rain and very damp conditions were the curse of the soldier and sportsman. When first made, this gun was fitted with two possibly identical barrels; after the top one was fired the sportsman set the cock to half cock, pushed the steel and combined pan cover forward, cleared the touch-hole, primed the pan and closed it. Pressure on the front of the trigger guard unlocked the barrels so that they could be rotated ready for the next shot.

At some time one barrel of this gun has been replaced by a similar shaped piece of Malacca cane, possibly as a result of damage, thereby making the gun much lighter, but also making it into a single barrelled gun. The owner, Sir Donald Cameron of Lochiel, has no idea when the barrel was removed.

'Gentle Lochiel', who was at Glenfinnan with his Cameron clansmen when the Prince's standard was raised, was a true and loyal supporter of the Jacobite cause. He carried with him into battle a pistol by Alexander Campbell of Doune. This is of a type made in steel with no trigger guard (a feature common to most Scottish firearms), with scroll, ram's-horn or claw butt. It has lost the silver pricker that should screw into the area between the scrolls of the butt. The pistol has all the signs of being well used, and would have been one of a pair.

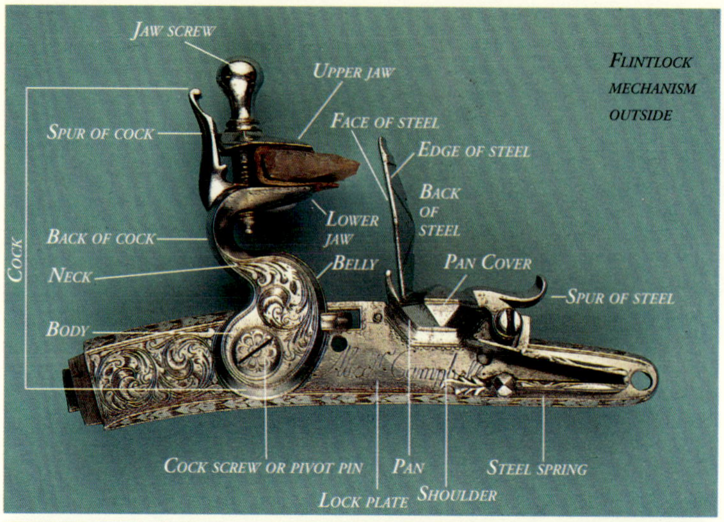

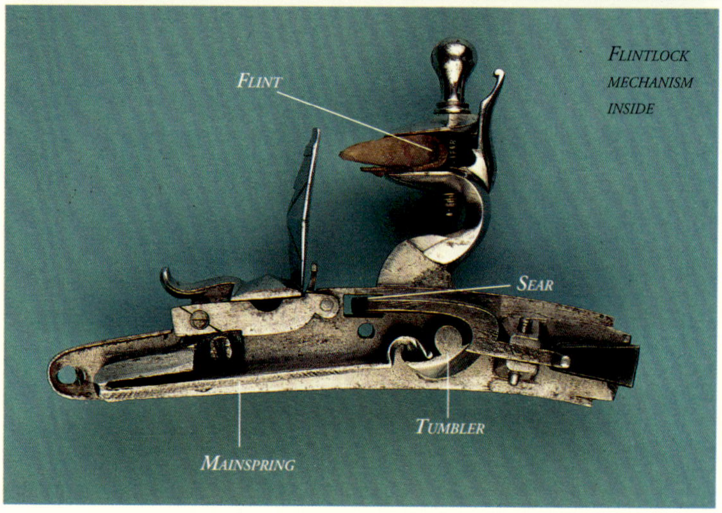

Belt hooks fitted to most Scottish pistols allowed them to be seen as part of the Highlander's dress, and also allowed for quick access: a belt pistol can be seen in the painting of David Tulloch of Dunbennen by Cosmo Alexander (page 91). Earlier Scottish pistols have right- and left-hand locks: later ones have locks on the right only.

A pair of pistols in the collection of The National Trust for Scotland at Brodick Castle, Isle of Arran, is also by Alexander Campbell of Doune and in fine condition. They are engraved with the crest of The Earl of Rochford on the silver escutcheons, and retain all their original fire-blueing to the stocks. They show no sign of wear. A pistol by this maker was taken at Culloden and is preserved in the Museum of Antiquities, Edinburgh.

All steel box-lock pistols are rare, and this pair by Segalas of London was taken from an English officer at the Battle of Prestonpans. To load this type of pistol the barrel is unscrewed at the breech and then primed with powder and ball. The barrel is then screwed back, the pan primed, the touch-hole cleared, flint checked and it is then ready to fire.

The service firearms issued to the British army in 1745 and used by foot soldiers and cavalry are well-made and robust; they are often signed by some of the leading gunmakers of the period, who would have been working to contracts from the Board of Ordnance. The barrels were made in advance and subjected to proofing by firing a larger than usual charge of black powder in the barrel. They were then viewed for any sign of distortion or cracking. If they passed proof they were stamped with view and proof marks, and stored until required. An impressive display of 700 service pistols can be seen in the armoury at Culzean Castle, South Ayrshire, and a unique collection of long land pattern muskets of the early eighteenth-century Argyll Militia is displayed at Inveraray Castle, Argyll.

Illustration of Government Soldier by Jenny Proudfoot

Comparison between the service firearms and the clansmen's weapons shows the unique design of the Scottish arms. An officer's fusil made for Lord William Gordon by Heriot of Edinburgh, with a barrel by James Barbar, a London maker of renown, shows an Anglo-Scottish weapon of military type but differing from the standard issue musket in that it has engraved decoration, a finer lock, and is lighter and better balanced. It would be supplied and paid for by the owner.

A foot soldier of the British army was equipped with a regulation long land pattern musket of .75 bore, with 24 cartridges (rounds). These saved time in action, prevented the wrong amount of powder being used and were quick and easy to use if the soldier was well trained. The cartridge was made of a tube of strong card-like paper, containing the measure of powder for the pan and breech plus the lead ball or bullet.

The pan was primed by pouring a small amount of powder from the cartridge. The end of the paper having been bitten off, the rest of the powder was then poured down the muzzle. The ball was rammed down, using the cartridge case as wadding.

General John Campbell wrote to his son Lt Col Jack Campbell:

'With regard to annition [sic] *which I find has been imbazelled or fired off without orders, the officers are to account to me for it, each cartrage at 1½d each flint at ditto ... I shall forward you some cases with cartrages and bags of ball in proportion – the cases with cartrages ought to be turned upside down every two or three days.'*[1]

Above left: General John Campbell, by Johnathan Richardson, and his son Lt. Col. Jack Campbell, by Thomas Gainsborough.

It was wise to ensure that no hot residue was left in the barrel prior to reloading, as this could result in severe injuries. It was practice to keep the muzzle away from the face and at arm's length when muzzle loading. A socket bayonet and a brass-hilted hanger sword completed the personal weapons of the British soldier who, alas, in 1745 could be fighting against members of his own family.

1 Fergusson, p 64.

Collectors and restorers

We have Geoffrey Jenkinson to thank, not only for suggesting the '45 Rising as the subject of an exhibition, but also for lending his impressive collection of Scottish swords. He has also lent an interesting targe that came from the renowned Keith Neal Collection.

William Keith Neal, by Andrew Festing.

William Keith Neal's important contribution to the study of historic weapons, together with his distinguished collection, has been carried on after his death in 1990 in the William Keith Neal Foundation, which he created. The history of British and European gunmakers and their output of weapons has been recorded in his many books written with co-author Major D H L Back.

A descendant of Earl Marischal Keith, Neal was very interested in Scottish weapons and was able to collect some of the finest available: they form a major part of this exhibition. Of particular relevance are the seventeenth-century English blunderbuss by Finch, taken at Culloden, and the Scottish long gun of traditional Highland form, of the type made for the Lairds of Grant, with paddle-shaped butt of fluted form and a snaphaunce lock dated 1680. The snaphaunce has a separate steel and pan cover; the flintlock combines these and is a refinement of the snaphaunce lock.

A fine Scottish pistol, signed D H, came from the collection of Richard Chapman, who repaired to perfection many pieces in the collection. In 1992, the year before he died, Richard Chapman wrote an excellent book on the restoration of antique firearms, and I am certain he would be pleased to know that Rodney French, the Trust's architectural metal worker, has used this book to make a replacement for the missing cock on the gun by Bourdiec and a top jaw and screw for the pistol by Mazallier, ensuring that the quality of Scottish craftsmanship is maintained.

The rare 1703 Scottish long gun by John Stuart is loaned by R T Gwynn, whose interest in arms and armour and in furniture of the medieval, Tudor and Stuart periods and related works of art began in the 1930s, and who has considerable knowledge in this field.

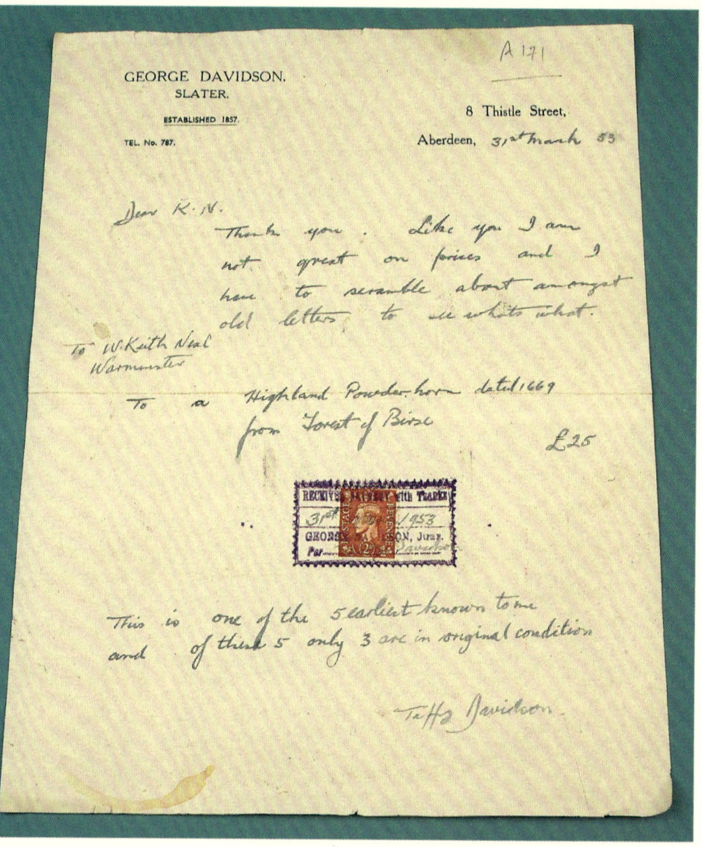

A 171

GEORGE DAVIDSON.
SLATER.
ESTABLISHED 1857.
TEL. No. 787.

8 Thistle Street,
Aberdeen, 31st March 53

Dear K. N.
Thank you. Like you I am not great on prices and I have to scramble about amongst old letters to see whats what.

To W. Keith Neal
Warminster

To a Highland Powder-horn dated 1669 from Forest of Birse

£25

RECEIVED PAYMENT with THANKS
31st 1953
GEORGE DAVIDSON, Junr.
Per ... Davidson

This is one of the 5 earliest known to me and of these 5 only 3 are in original condition

Taffy Davidson

A receipt for a 1669 powder flask (No 6:5).

Although they do not form part of the exhibition, the pair of Scottish all-brass snaphaunce belt pistols by James Low of Dundee is included in this catalogue because of its rarity and unique place in the development of Scottish weapons. The pistols have extending stocks of steel rod, threaded to lock in the extended position. The lemon-shaped butts unscrew to form a butt extension, perhaps making them more accurate. They are of the finest quality; James Low was renowned for his superb workmanship. A fine all-brass gun with extendable stock (LH419) by Low is in the collection of the Museum of Antiquities, Edinburgh.

Detail of an English blunderbuss by Finch (No 5:3).

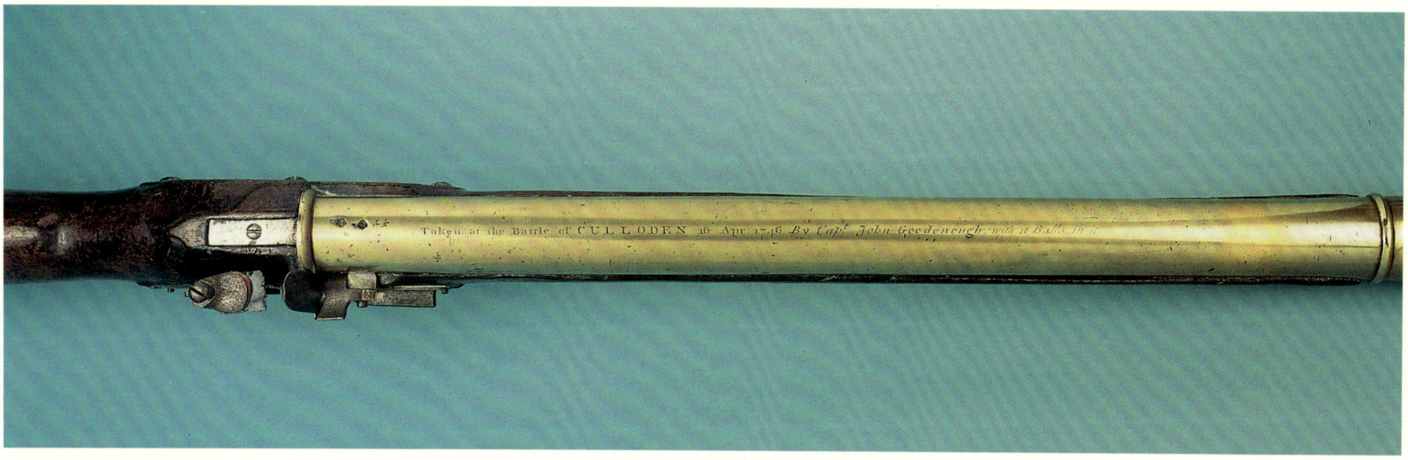

THE EXHIBITS

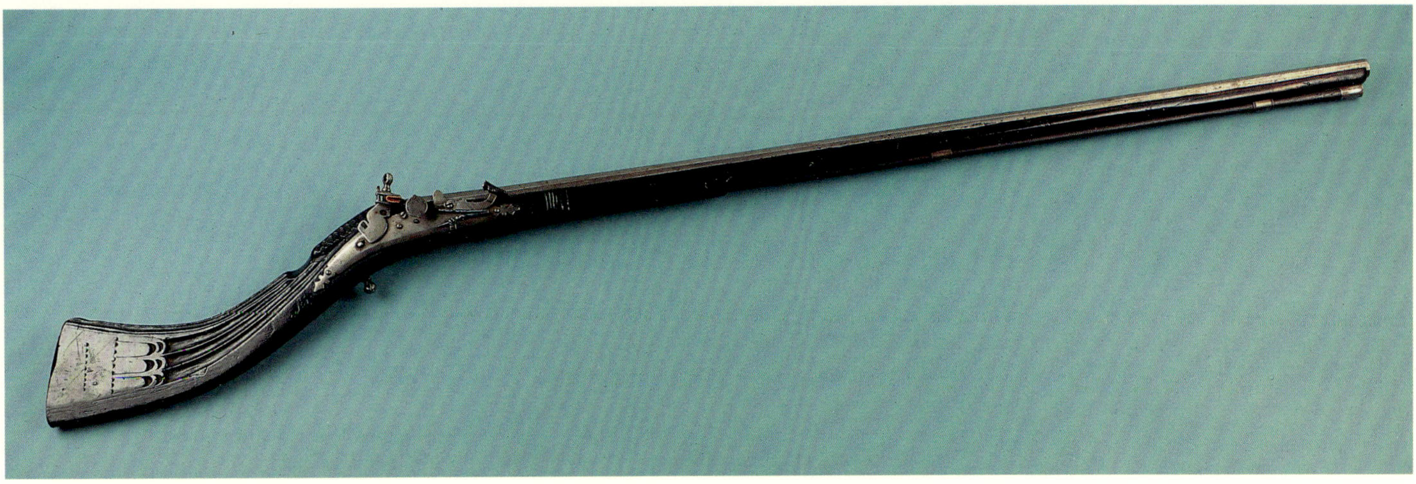

5:1 Scottish late 17th-century snaphaunce fowling piece

Typical Highland form, the paddle-shaped butt with deeply fluted full stock, the underside of the plain barrel signed with the initials R A N. The lock dated 1685 on the fence. It has full-cock position only. 62" long.

The gun was at one time in the Royal Collection and was presented to the Scottish United Services Museum, Edinburgh Castle, by King Edward VII.

Lender: Private Collection.

Literature: Neal & Back, *Gunmakers 1540-1740,* p 203; Woosnam-Savage; Woosnam-Savage & Blair.

5:2 Scottish early 18th-century flintlock musket or fowling piece

The lock engraved I Stuart, the long barrel with IOHN STUART 1703 engraved at the breech. Engraved brass trigger guard, ramrod pipes butt and side plate, the full walnut stock carved with a form of acanthus leaf at the toe of the butt. 62½" long.

John Stuart was gunmaker to the Lairds of Clan Grant: see also 5:11. This is the only known Scottish long-gun of conventional European form made between 1700 and 1745. A pair of pistols formerly in the possession of the Countess of Seafield is signed John Stuart on locks of identical form.

Lender: R T Gwynn.

Literature: Woosnam-Savage; Woosnam-Savage & Blair.

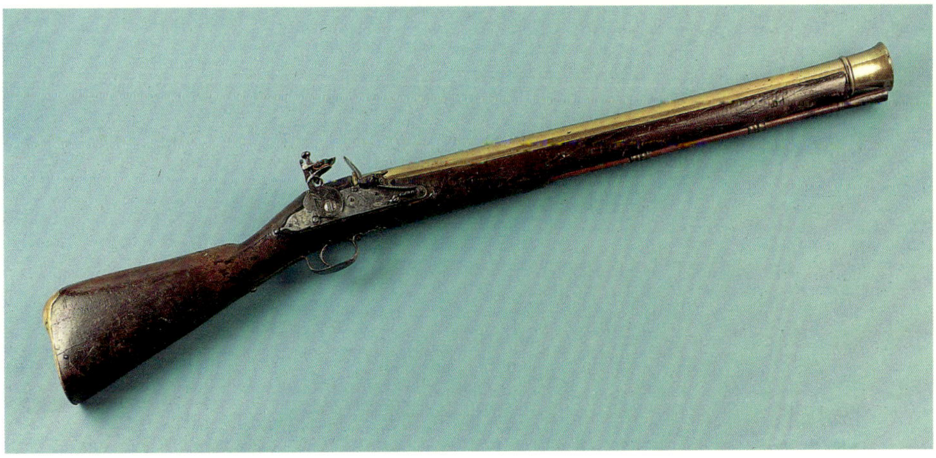

5:3 English late 17th-century flintlock dog lock blunderbuss

The lock engraved with typical foliate scrolls above the I FINCH signature. The heavy brass barrel is London proofed and bears the maker's mark I FINCH, with the engraved inscription, *Taken at the battle of CULLODEN 16th APRIL 1746 by Capt John Goodenough with 18 balls in it.* c1670. 38" long.

John Finch served as an assistant to the court of the Gunmakers Company when it was formed in 1638.

Lender: William Keith Neal Foundation.

Literature: Neal & Back, *Gunmakers 1540-1740,* pp 151-3.

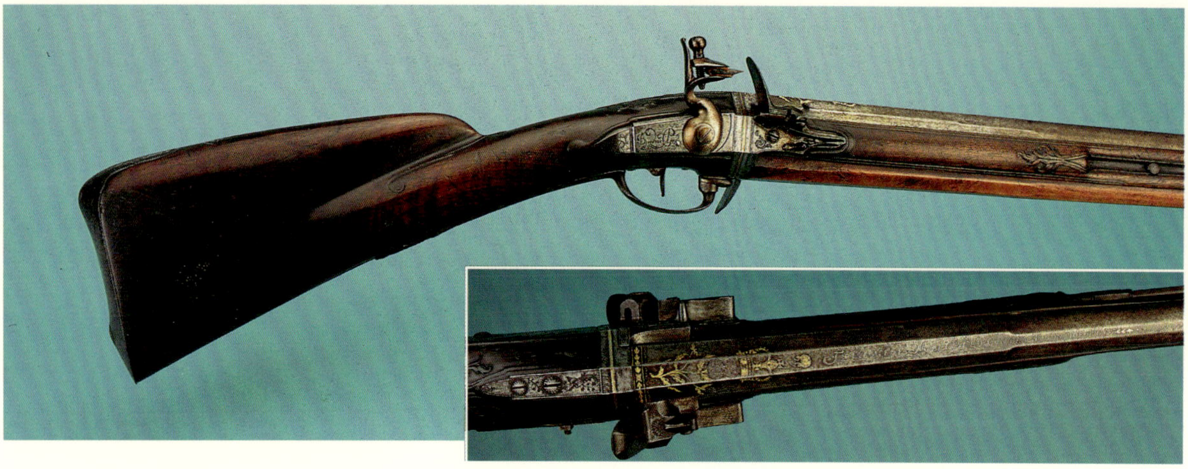

David Wemyss, Lord Elcho

5:4 Early 18th-century French turn-about or wender flintlock fowling-piece

The lock engraved BOURDIEC PARIS, the three-stage barrel inlaid with a gold thistle surmounted by a royal crown, with a gold shell forming part of an inscription from Virgil's *Aeneid* V i 95.6:
TU:NE:CEDE:MALIS:SED:CONTRA:AUDENTIOR:ITO: (QUA:TUA:TE:FORTUNA:SINET)
(As for you, don't give way to evil: on the contrary venture forth more boldly on the route which your destiny permits). This quotation (the Sybil urging Aeneas to acts of greater daring), is also seen on Jacobite portrait glass. One barrel replaced by a wooden replica, perhaps because of damage or to lighten the gun. The steel furniture engraved with trophies and scrolls. Walnut full stock. *c*1730. 61¼" long.

The replacement flint-cock was made in The National Trust for Scotland's workshop by Rodney French, 1995.

The gun was given to Lord Elcho by Prince Charles Edward Stuart and was subsequently bequeathed to Cameron of Lochiel by Francis Lord Elcho, son of the 7th Earl of Wemyss, in 1808. It possibly belonged to the Prince's father, King James VIII, the Old Pretender: this would explain the device of the crown above the thistle rather than the Prince of Wales's feathers. There are many recorded instances of the Prince using a sporting gun.

Lender: Sir Donald Cameron of Lochiel.

Lt Col Jack Campbell, by Thomas Gainsborough.

5:5 Argyll Militia short land pattern flintlock musket

Engraved with royal crown, tower, and dated 1742 on the lock, the barrel with view and proof marks, initials A G on the breech. Fitted with iron sling swivels, ramrod, and socket bayonet. The butt plate trigger guard and ramrod pipes are of brass. 42" barrel.

The Argyll Militia under the command of Lt Col Jack Campbell of Mamore was raised from Clan Campbell and was loyal to King George.

Lender: The Duke of Argyll (Inveraray Castle).

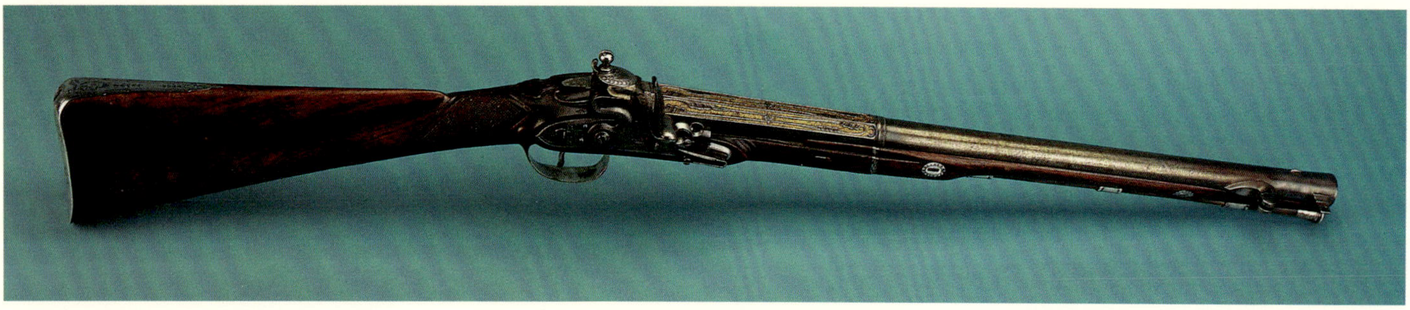

5:6 Silver mounted mid-18th-century flintlock officer's cavalry carbine

The two-stage barrel octagonal at the breech, the matted chiselled decoration inlaid with gold. The full walnut stock with fine chequering and carved shell at the breech. The whalebone ramrod with silver tip; the bayonet is missing. The engraving is crude and the hallmarks spurious. This carbine has many features that indicate an English gunmaker working in the colonies. 10 bore. 37" long.

Known as the carbine of Ensign Home. William Home, Cornet in Lord Balmerino's Regiment of Life Guards, carried the regimental standard at Culloden, was taken prisoner and condemned at Carlisle. Reprieved on account of his youth, he was exiled to the Continent, where he rose to the rank of colonel in Frederick the Great's Prussian army. Returning to Scotland in 1774, he died in 1794 and was buried in Edrom Kirk, Berwickshire.

Lender: The National Trust for Scotland (Culloden).

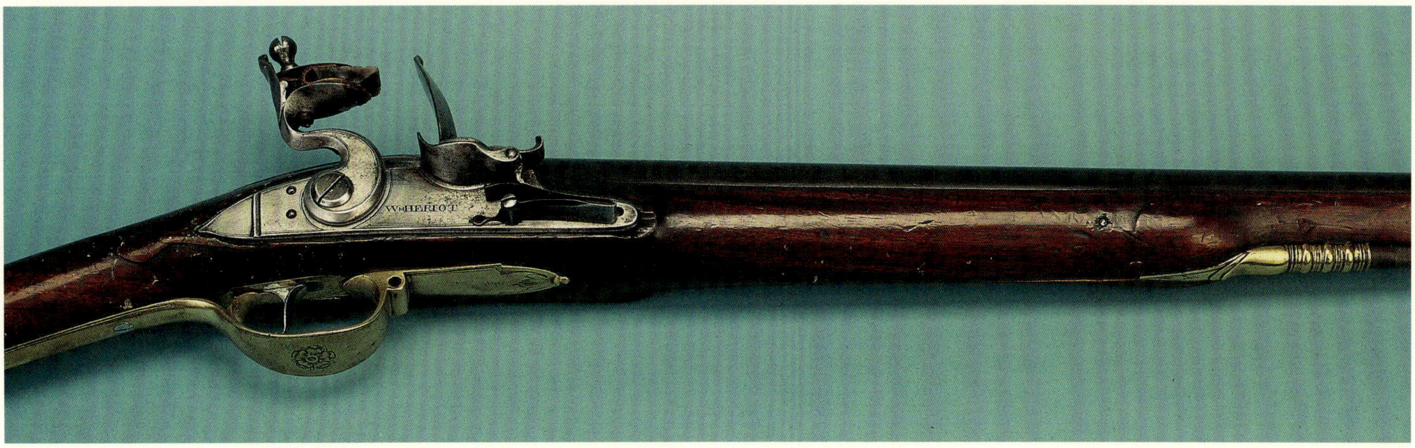

5.7 Early 18th-century flintlock officer's fusil

Signed W Heriot on the lock, the barrel signed Barber. Full walnut stock, with four brass baluster-turned ramrod pipes. The brass butt plate engraved Ld Wm Gordon, Lt Col. *c*1740. 12 bore. 55" long.

A good example of an Edinburgh gunmaker, William Heriot, mounting a London barrel by an earlier maker.

The owner of this gun, Lord William Gordon, was a babe in arms in 1746 when his mother, the Duchess of Gordon, had to watch the Jacobite army violate her home, Gordon Castle, at Fochabers.

Lender: The National Trust for Scotland (Brodie Castle).

Literature: Whitelaw, *Scottish Arms Makers*, pp 148-9.

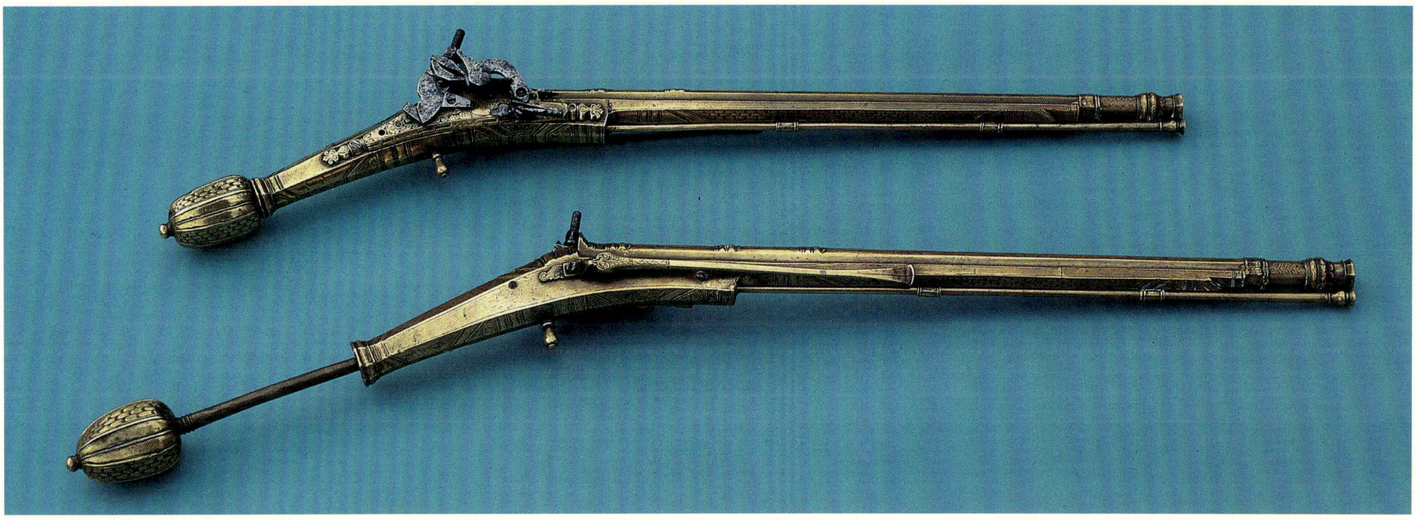

5:8 Pair of rare Scottish snaphaunce all-brass belt pistols by James Low of Dundee

Dated 1614 at the breech and with right- and left-hand locks. The octagonal lemon-shaped butts have the unique feature of extension bars. The butts are extended by unscrewing them and locked by screwing them back a turn. The trigger pull can be adjusted by means of a screw which passes through the lock plate and puts pressure on the sear. This is the earliest known example of this device used throughout the muzzle loading period. These are the earliest known dated Scottish lemon butt pistols and confirm the skill and ingenuity of the maker. *c*1614. 23" extending to 27" long.

Not exhibited. Collection of R T Gwynn.

Literature: Whitelaw, *Scottish Arms Makers*; Caldwell (ed), p 30; Woosnam-Savage, 'Scottish Long Guns'; Woosnam Savage & Blair, p 43.

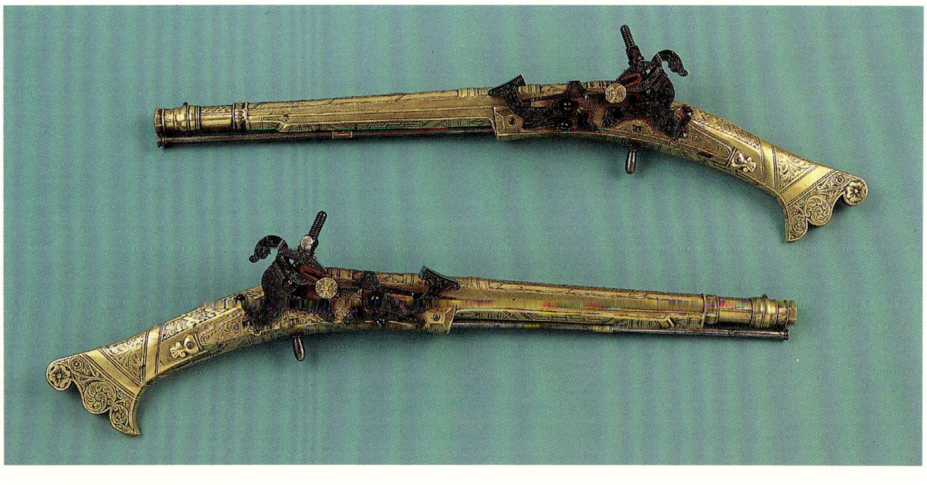

5:9 Pair of Scottish snaphaunce all-brass belt pistols

By James Low of Dundee, dated 1619 on the breech of each barrel and on the fence, left- and right-hand locks (both replaced), the butts of fish-tail form engraved with floral panels, the barrels with a blank shield. 16 1/2" long.

Lender: The William Keith Neal Foundation.

Literature: Whitelaw, *Scottish Arms Makers*, p 50; Neal and Back, *Gunmakers 1540-1740.*

5:10 *Pair of Scottish snaphaunce pistols with steel barrels*

They are elaborately inlaid with silver decoration in the form of rosettes and flowers. There is also a large silver plaque engraved with the owner's crest, a crown with feathers emerging above, and three silver discs with bars of silver complete the ornamentation. The pistols have their locks arranged on the right- and left-hand side for convenience when wearing on a belt. The lockplates are decorated with rosettes, foliage and a cable design and have the maker's mark, A L with a hammer and crown above, stamped near the centre.

The steel stock is inlaid with silver bands decorated en suite with the rest of the pistol. The butts are of unusual form, being shaped like a pommel but slightly oval. Both the ball triggers and prickers are overlaid with silver and engraved, and the long belt hooks are also inlaid with silver. *c*1645. 22 bore. 19" long.

Lender: The William Keith Neal Foundation.

Literature: Neal & Back, *Gunmakers,1540-1740,* pp 85-87; Whitelaw, *Scottish Arms Makers*, p 73.

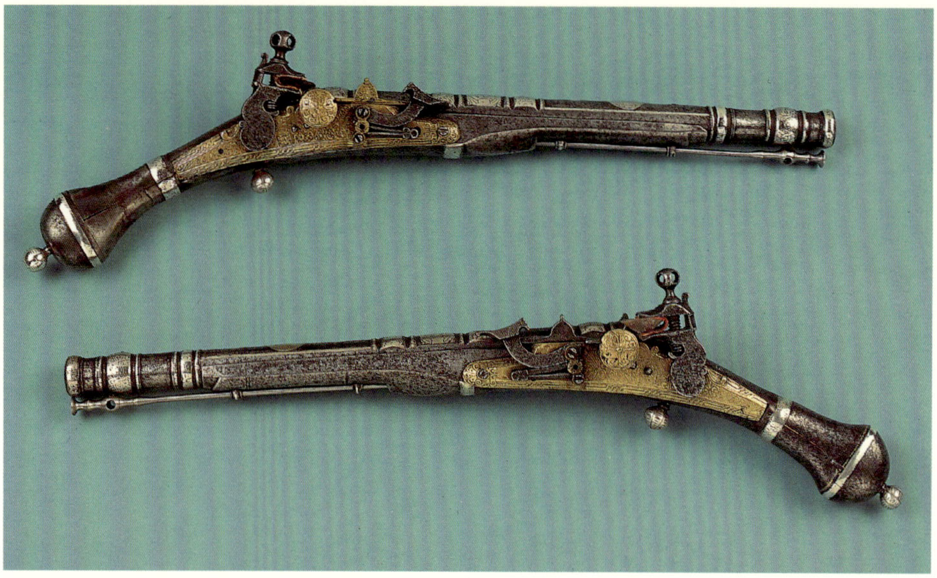

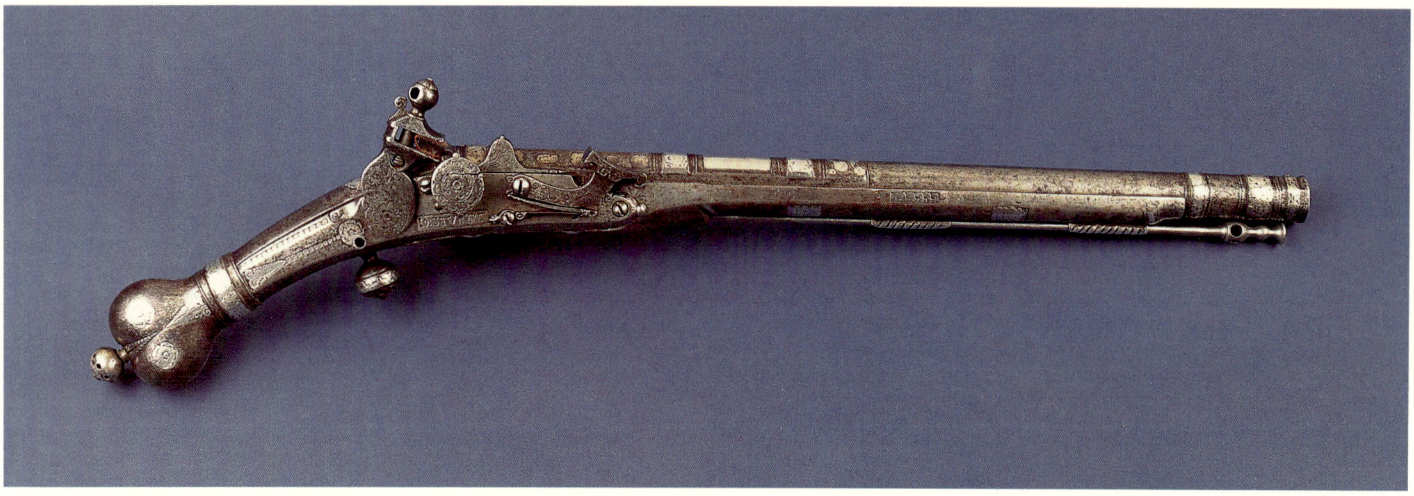

5:11 *Scottish steel and silver snaphaunce belt pistol*

Signed Io Stvart on the lock. Dated 1672 in silver inlaid panel at the breech, the barrel decorated with silver raised bands, the heart-shaped butt with engraved roses of silver, a band of silver on the ball trigger, the pricker ball of pierced silver. 20$^{1}/_{2}$" long.

John Stuart was gunmaker to the Lairds of Grant: see also 5:2.

Lender: The William Keith Neal Foundation.

Literature: Whitelaw, *Scottish Arms Makers*.

5:12 *Scottish all-steel, scroll-butt flintlock belt pistol*

Signed H W on the lock, the barrel with five raised silver bands engraved with rosettes and leaves. The engraved cock has a dog catch which acts as a safety catch, the steel stock with early form of scroll butt. *c*1670. 18 bore. 21" long.

Pistols of this type are also known as dags.

Lender: The William Keith Neal Foundation.

Literature: Neal & Back, *Gunmakers 1540-1740* p 154; Whitelaw, *Scottish Arms Makers*, p 281.

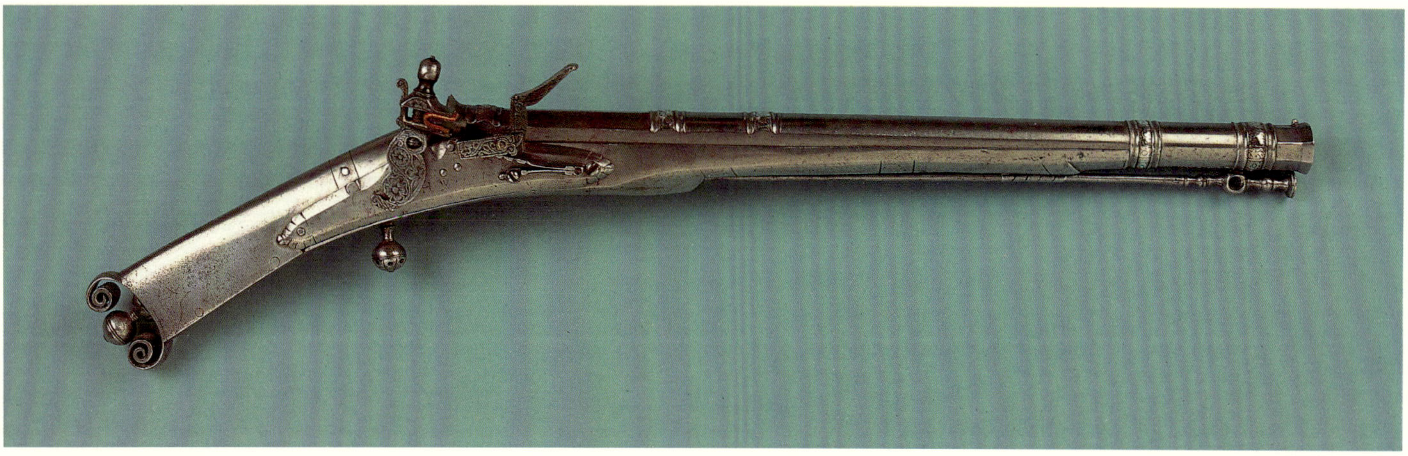

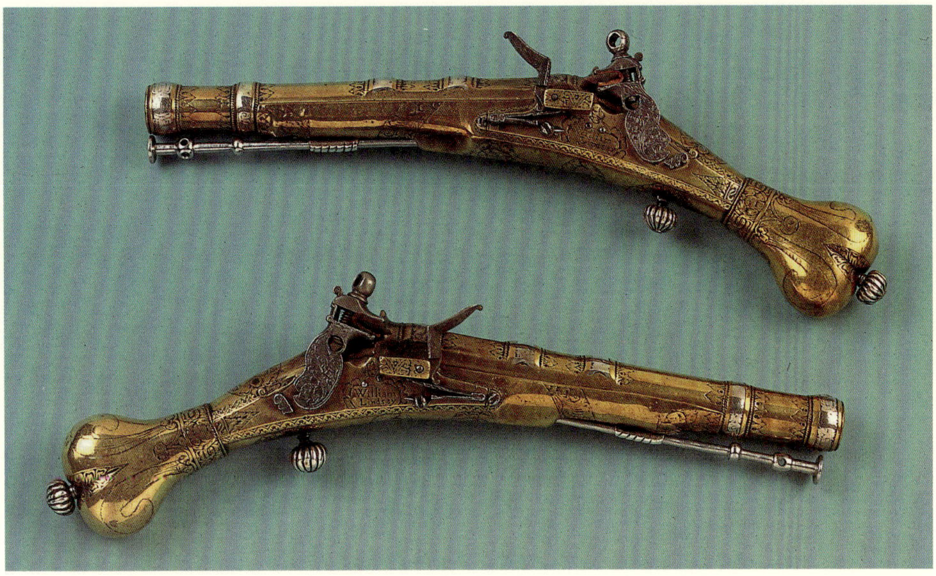

5:13 *Pair of Scottish brass and silver flintlock belt pistols*

The engraved steel cocks with a safety catch, acting on the full cock position with silver triggers, prickers and raised bands on the barrels. The heart butts engraved with two ostrich plumes out of a ducal coronet, the crest of Lord Scrope of Bolton Castle. Signed William Lindsay on the locks within a cartouche of engraved leaves. The engraved rifled barrels – a rare feature on Scottish pistols – are 48 bore. *c*1695. 9" long.

Lender: The William Keith Neal Foundation.

Literature: Whitelaw, *Scottish Arms Makers*, p 23.

5:14 *Scottish steel and silver flintlock belt pistol*

The lock signed with the engraved initals D H. The lock, stock and barrel with fine engraving and silver inlay, the heart butt also with silver inlay. Brass pricker, trigger,and belt hook which has a finely cut and pierced disc. The flint cock is of elegant form with a peascod shaped steel. *c*1720. 17 bore. 16" long.

Whitelaw records an Elgin maker with the initials D H (David Harison, gunmaker, 1757).

Lender: The William Keith Neal Foundation.

Literature: Whitelaw, *Scottish Arms Makers*; Caldwell (ed), p 214.

5:15 *Scottish steel and silver flintlock belt pistol*

Signed John Campbell Downe [Doune] on the lock, the scroll butt inlaid with silver stars (almost identical decoration is found on the sword hilts of John Allan of Stirling), a silver shield behind the breech engraved with the arms of Cowper. The belt hook with pierced side plate, the trigger and pricker of pierced and engraved silver. The barrel engraved at the muzzle and breech with scroll decoration. *c*1690. 24 bore. 16 1/4" long.

John Campbell, senior, was apprenticed to Thomas Caddell (see 5:16).

Lender: The William Keith Neal Foundation.

Literature: Whitelaw, *Scottish Arms Makers*, p 42.

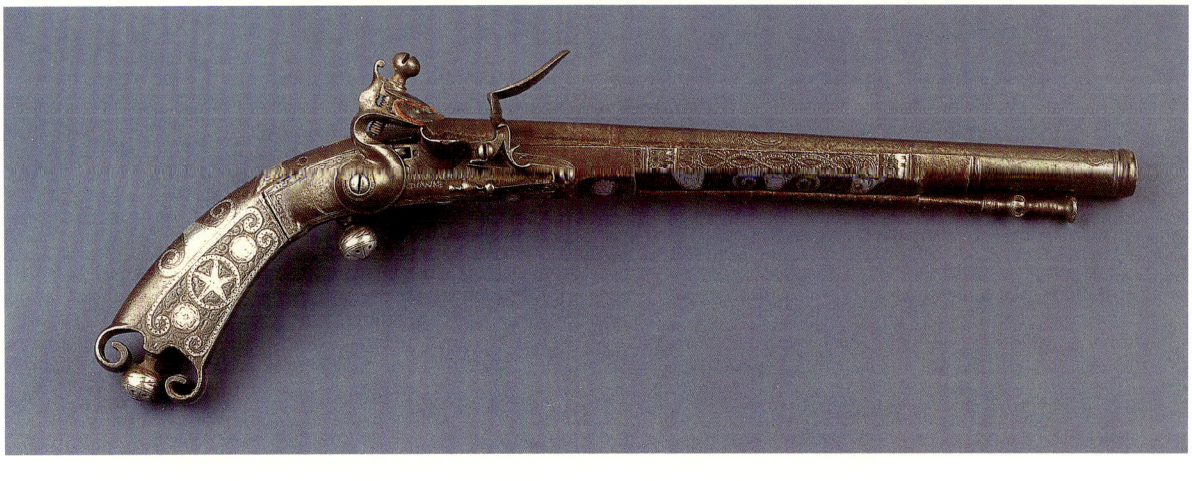

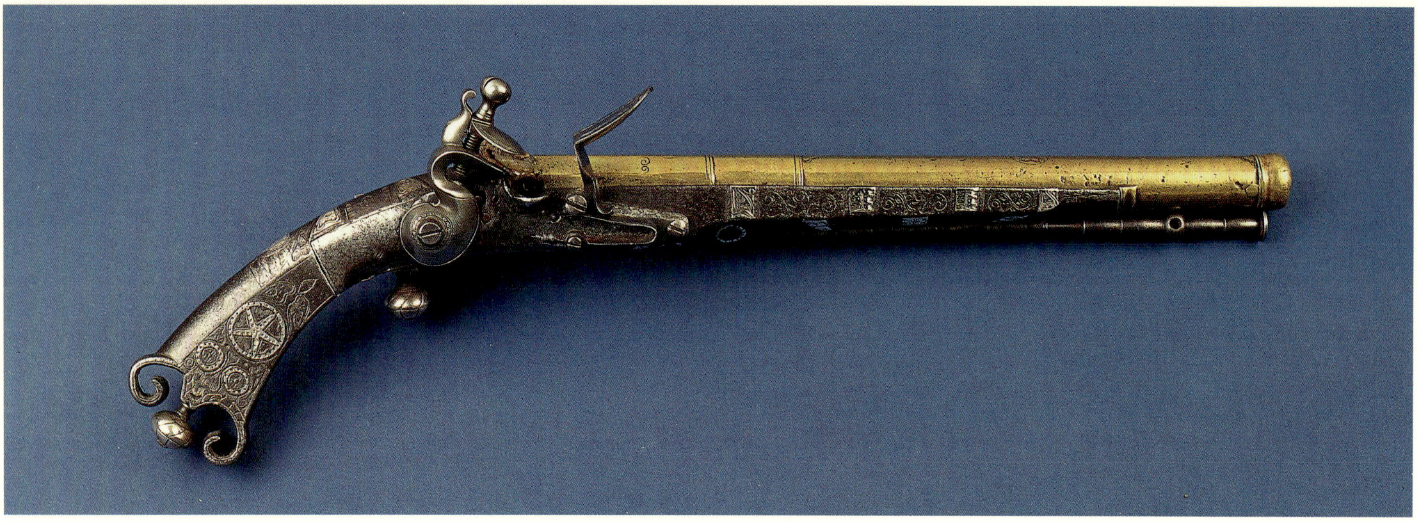

5:16 Scottish flintlock belt pistol

The lock signed Caddell, the all-steel stock inlaid with silver bands with engraved rose heads, the scroll butt with silver stars, a three-stage brass barrel engraved with floral decoration. The trigger and pricker of engraved silver. The cock is a replacement. *c*1715. 27 bore. 15 3/4" long.

The Caddell family produced four pistol makers, all called Thomas. The elder had his workshop in Muthill near Drummond Castle, stronghold of the Jacobite Duke of Perth. He later moved to Doune in Stirlingshire, where he became renowned for his skill.

Lender: The William Keith Neal Foundation.

Literature: Whitelaw, *Scottish Arms Makers*.

5:17 Scottish steel and brass flintlock belt pistol

With scroll butt inlaid with silver stars and scroll decoration, the stock with similar silver inlay. The belt hook with pierced tang, a three-stage brass barrel inlaid with silver at the octagonal breech and with incised lines forward of the breech. Trigger and pricker of pierced silver. *c*1720. 36 bore. 16 3/4" long.

Said to have belonged to James Boswell, and came from Malahide Castle, Dublin.

Lender: The William Keith Neal Foundation.

Literature: Whitelaw, *Scottish Arms Makers*.

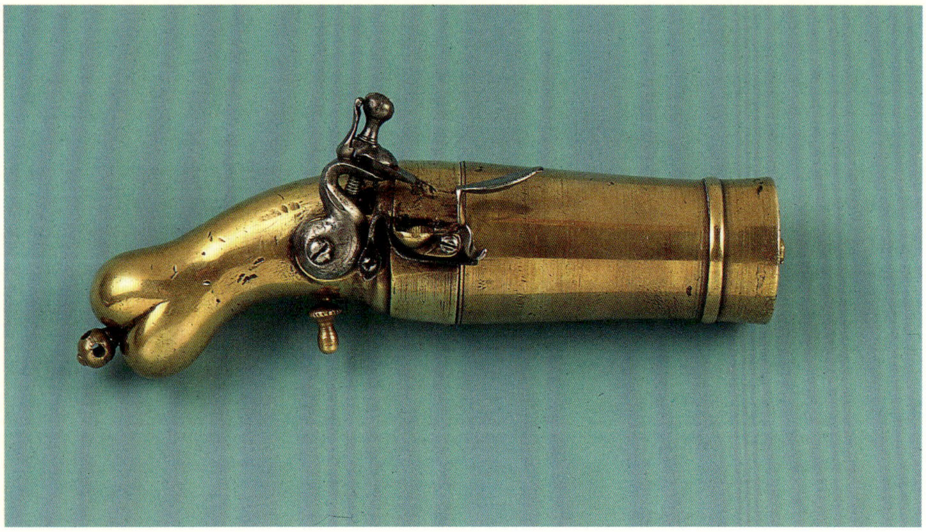

5:18 Rare Scottish all-brass four-shot flintlock revolver

With heart butt and iron pricker, the heavy cast brass barrel block with four chambers. The plain stock and barrel of pale high quality brass. The barrel is rotated by hand after each shot. *c*1700. 36 bore. 8 1/2" long.

Lender: The William Keith Neal Foundation.

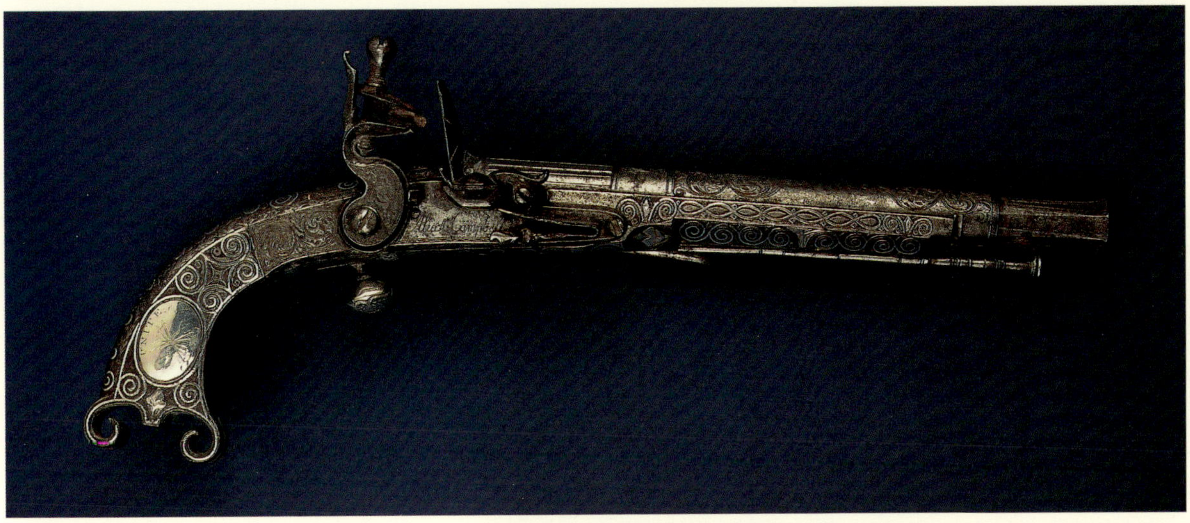

Donald Cameron of Lochiel, by an unknown artist.

5:19 Scottish steel and silver flintlock belt pistol

By Alexander Campbell of Doune. The scroll butt with silver escutcheon engraved with the crest of five arrows and motto 'Unite, for Cameron of Lochiel'. The reverse engraved with the intertwined cypher of Ls. The steel stock decorated with typical inlaid silver scroll work of the Doune makers, also seen on inlaid Scottish basket hilts by the Allan family of Stirling. It could be the work of the same craftsmen. *c*1740. 12½" long.

Lender: Sir Donald Cameron of Lochiel.

Literature: Whitelaw, *Scottish Arms Makers*, p 42.

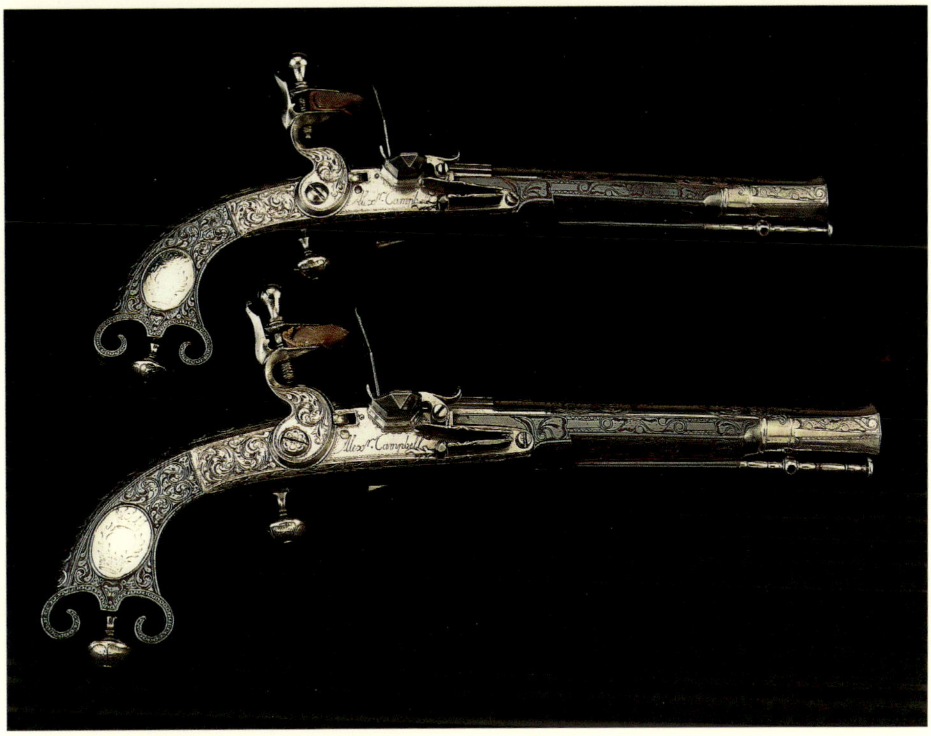

5:20 Fine pair of Scottish steel and silver flintlock belt pistols

By Alexander Campbell of Doune. The silver escutcheons are engraved with the arms of The Earl of Rochford, the steel stocks fire-blued with silver bands and profusely decorated with foliate engraving, the barrels in two stages fluted at the breech with flared octagonal muzzles. The belt hooks have pierced tangs, silver triggers and prickers. *c*1740. 12" long.

These pistols were made for William Henry Nassau, 4th Earl of Rochford, 1717-81. A pistol by this maker taken at Culloden is displayed in the *Dynasty* exhibition, Scottish National Portrait Gallery, Edinburgh.

Lender: The National Trust for Scotland (Brodick Castle).

Literature: Whitelaw, *Scottish Arms Makers.*

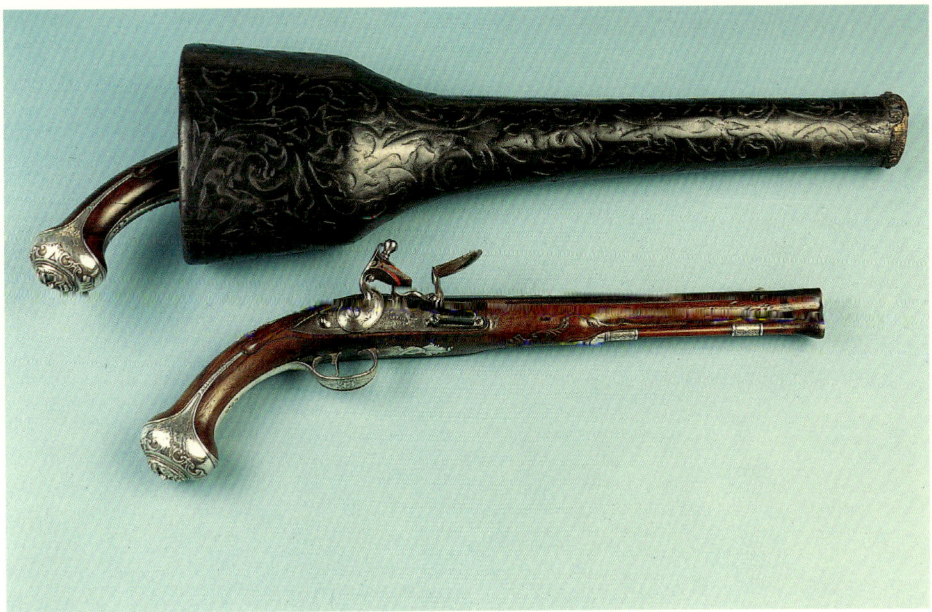

5:21 Pair of silver-mounted holster pistols

By Benjamin Griffin, the barrels signed in gold, Griffin, Bond Street, London. The breeches chiselled on a gold background, with blued barrels, marked with London proof and Griffin mark. The full walnut stocks are carved with shells, the silver mounts are hallmarked for 1745 and carry the maker's mark of J A (Jeremiah Ashley). The cast silver side plates with reclining sportsman, dog, gun and dead game. The escutcheons are engraved with the crest and cypher of Lord Fitzalan, eldest son the Duke of Norfolk. 17 bore. 11½" long.

These pistols epitomise the best quality horse or holster pistols of the period and would have been carried only by the highest ranks in the field.

Lender: The William Keith Neal Foundation.

Literature: Neal & Back, *Griffin, Tow & Bailes*, pp 92-3.

The Duke of Cumberland: engraving by unknown artist

5:22 *Pair of all-steel box lock flintlock turn-off cannon-barrelled travelling pistols*

The locks engraved Segalas, London, within rococo cartouches. The tops of both the cocks damaged. *c*1740. 13" long.

Israel Segalas, junior, was born in 1714 and apprenticed to Lewis Barbar on 27 March 1729.

These pistols were owned by a British officer who was captured at the Battle of Prestonpans. The cocks were deliberately broken to render them useless: they were then returned to him.

Lender: Sir Donald Cameron of Lochiel.

Literature: Neal & Back, *Gunmakers 1540-1740.*

5:23 *French silver-mounted flintlock holster pistol*

Signed Mazelier Aparis on the engraved lock. The fire-blued barrel decorated with gold masks, scrolls and a Roman centurion at the breech, the silver mounts parcel-gilt-chased in low relief. The steel is chiselled with a grotesque mask, and the tail of the pan cover is formed as a dolphin. A cast silver escutcheon is in the form of the coat-of-arms of the Duc de Fraser. The motto *Ie suis prest* is inlaid in gold at the muzzle, the burr walnut stock carved with masks and foliate decoration. It is possible that this pistol was presented by King James VIII to Lord Lovat during his exile in France. *c*1740. 28 bore. 21" long.

A replacement top jaw and screw made in The National Trust for Scotland workshop by Rodney French, July 1995.

Simon Fraser, 11th Lord Lovat, the Chief of Clan Fraser, was created Duc de Fraser by the Old Pretender whilst in exile in Paris. Simon the Fox, as he was known, was captured on an island in Loch Morar after the defeat at Culloden, taken to London, tried, forfeited and beheaded on Tower Hill in 1747 – the last nobleman to be executed in this way.

Lender: Mackintosh of Mackintosh (Moy Hall).

Literature: Mann, p 577; Wallace Collection Catalogue.

Simon Fraser, Lord Lovat: engraving after William Hogarth.

5:24 *Pair of Scottish heart-butt steel and silver flintlock belt pistols*

The locks fitted with safety catches signed Jas McRay. The silver inlay comprising hearts, bands and wavy lines with a royal crown behind the backsite. The pierced prickers designed to be unscrewed by using the steel ramrod as a lever. The belt hooks with a series of rings ending with a fish-tail at the butt, *c*1725. The locks replaced *c*1745. 28 bore. 11" long.

Almost certainly made by James Mackenzie of Dundee.

Traditionally known as Prince Charles Edward Stuart's pistols.

From the collection of Lord Lovat.

Lender: Mrs Ann Gloag (Beaufort Castle).

5:25 *A pair of flintlock heavy dragoon government service holster pistols*

Signed Jordan and dated 1742, with brass spurred pommels, trigger guards, side plates and ramrod pipes. The ramrods a later replacement. The locks engraved with the royal crown. 20 bore. 19" long.

Pistols of this type were made by various gunmakers under licence from and the strict control of the Board of Ordnance. They are part of a large collection of service pistols formed by the first Marquis of Ailsa for the West Lowland Fencible Regiment.

Lender: The National Trust for Scotland (Culzean Castle).

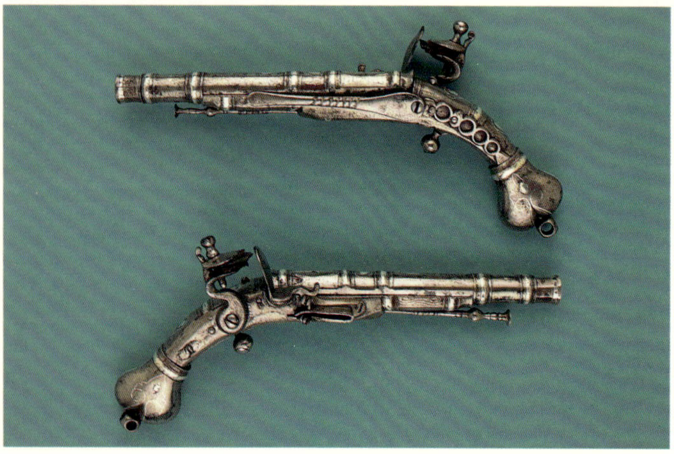

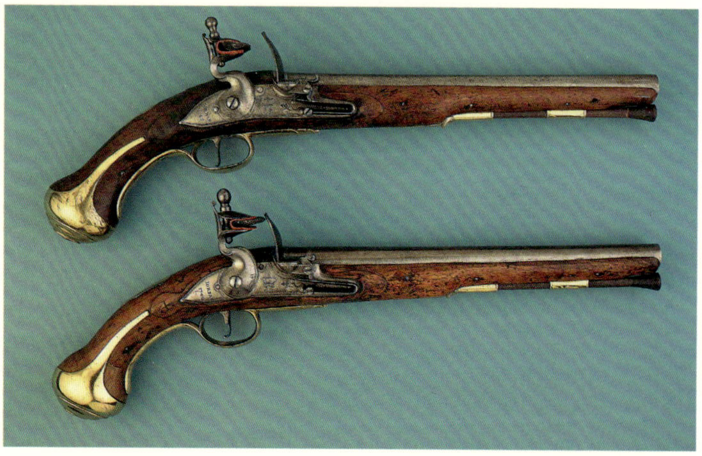

Scottish Powder Horns

By Jackie Moran

In the seventeenth century a specifically Scottish type of powder horn was developed and remained popular into the eighteenth century. These powder horns were made from cowhorn softened by heat and flattened to give two broad surfaces. Typically, the powder horns are decorated all over, front and back. The broad base of the horn is closed with a wooden plug held in place by iron or copper alloy nails. This was a permanent fixture and was not removed for filling the horn. The point of the horn was cut away to form a nozzle for pouring the powder. This was often reinforced with a mount made of pewter and the nozzle itself was shut with a stopper normally made of wood. Very few of these stoppers survive. Most powder horns were made with lugs, loops or holes so that they could be suspended over the shoulder on a cord.

There is almost no information on the makers of powder horns. Occasionally horners are mentioned in the Scottish burghs but it seems unlikely that this is where we should look for the manufacture of most of them. Interlace patterns and designs including spotted animals feature prominently on powder horns. These motifs are characteristic of other items such as dirks, targes and brooches etc, made by craftsmen working in or on the edge of the Highlands. By and large these motifs were not used by town-based craftsmen like gunsmiths and goldsmiths.

Fortunately a great number of powder horns have dates incorporated in their decoration, mainly the 1670s, 80s and 90s. In most cases it is obvious that the date is part of the scheme of decoration carved by the horner rather than a secondary carving added by the new owner. A number of powder horns have initals as well as dates carved on them. The horner was presumably required by the purchaser to put his initials, and sometimes his coat-of-arms, in the design. However, some of the initials may well be those of the maker, particularly when two sets are present, although this is very uncommon.

Charles E Whitelaw, the great collector and historian of Scottish weapons, favoured a classification system for powder horns:

TYPE A: Horns with their surface divided up by cross bands of interlace and fan ornament, with one or two square or oblong panels.

TYPE B: Horns with ornament enclosed within circles and consisting of interlace, geometric patterns, etc.

TYPE C: A combination of types A and B.

TYPE D: Horns ornamented usually with three panels enclosing the Scottish thistle, English rose and Dutch tulip.

TYPE E: Horns with hunting scenes, a house, leaf scrolls etc.

TYPE F: Horns with simple geometric designs of dashes or zig-zag lines.

The majority of surviving horns appear to be of types A-C, and especially A. After 1700 the quality of the decoration on powder horns very quickly deteriorates, the first sign of this being the use of a compass in producing interlaced designs.

The failure of the Jacobite Rising is often seen as the main cause of the demise of the Scottish targe, sword and pistol-making industries, not least because their use in the country was prohibited by law. The manufacture of powder horns could well have been affected in the same way; also, cheaper English or foreign horns or flasks were becoming more readily available.

Since powder horns appear to have been made by rural craftsmen in or on the fringes of the Highlands, changes in Highland society in the early eighteenth century may have lessened the demand for these items or discouraged their production. The manufacture of dirks and brass ring brooches showed a similar decline at this time.

THE EXHIBITS

6:1 Scottish undecorated, flattened cowhorn powder horn

Taken at Culloden. *c*1730. 8" long.

Lender: The Duke of Atholl (Blair Castle).

6:2 Large Scottish flattened cowhorn powder horn

Decorated with incised traditional decoration. *c*1690. 1'3" long.

Lender: Ian Grant of Glenmoriston.

6:3 Scottish flattened cowhorn powder horn

The nozzle with pierced pewter mount and typical incised decoration, dated 1669. 10" long.

Lender: The William Keith Neal Foundation.

6:4 Scottish flattened cowhorn powder horn of typical form

Incised decoration with the initials A M K. *c*1700. 11" long.

Lender: The William Keith Neal Foundation.

6:5 Scottish flattened cowhorn powder horn of typical Highland form and decoration

Showing signs of much use with missing wooden base plug. *c*1700. 10" long.

Lender: The William Keith Neal Foundation.

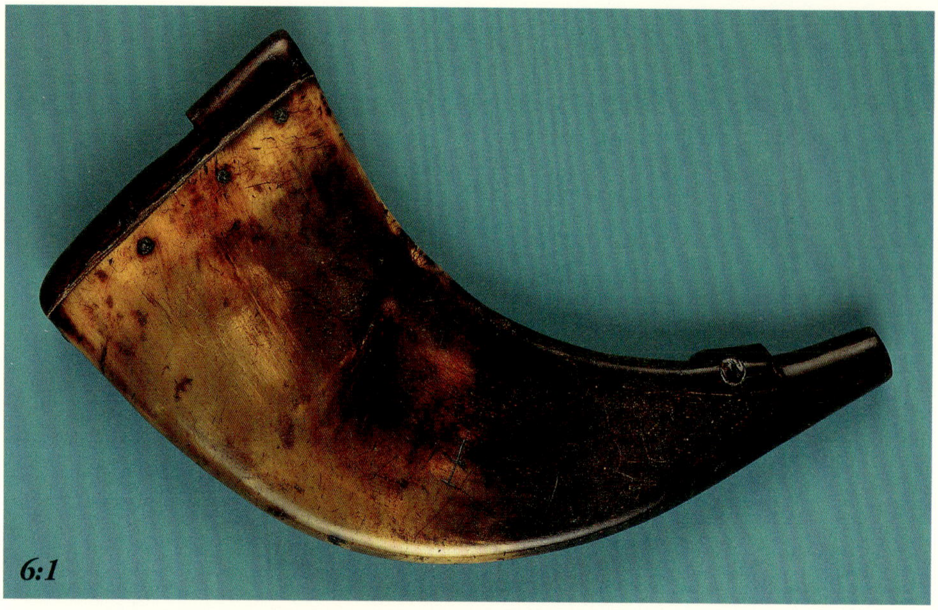

6:1

6:2

6:3

6:4

6:5

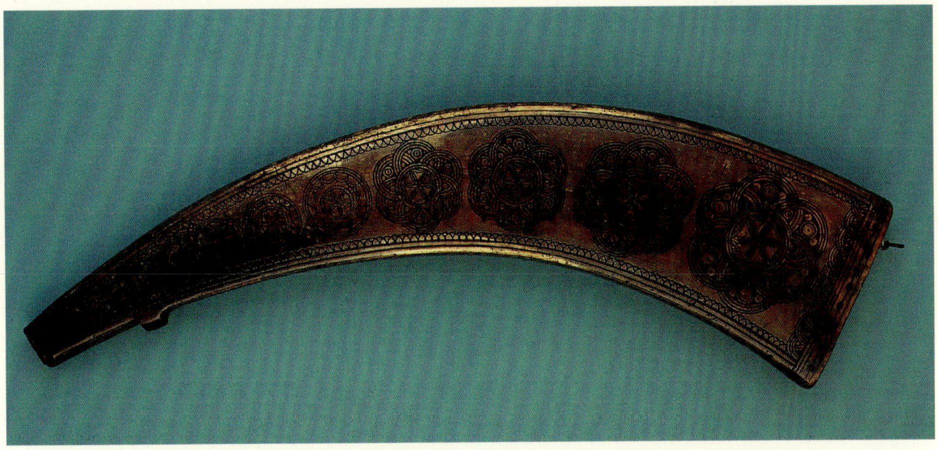

6:6 Large Scottish flattened cowhorn powder horn

Decorated with incised traditional decoration. *c*1690. 1'3" long.

Lender: Drambuie Ltd.

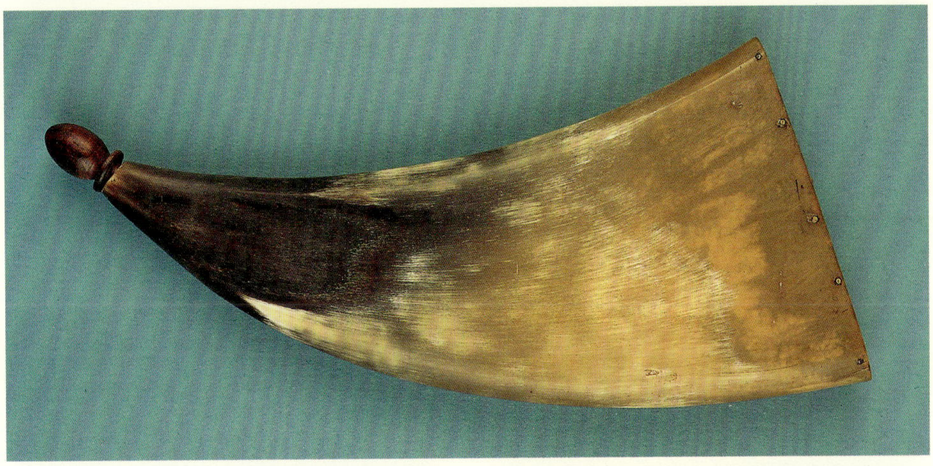

6:7 Scottish flattened cowhorn powder horn

Of a plain type made for the pocket as it has no loops or holes to suspend it by a cord. The stopper is of later date. *c*1740. 7" long.

Lender: Private collection.

6:8 Scottish early 18th-century cowhorn powder horn

Inscribed 1723 James Inos on one side and on the reverse, *A whiter horn ye do not ken JAMES INOS is my master name.* Dated 1723. 8" long.

Lender: John Kirk.

6:9. Hardened black leather powder flask of 2lb capacity

The brass cap unscrews to form a powder measure. *c*1745. 10" high.

Lender: Private collection.

Literature: Neal & Back, *Gunmakers, their trade cards.*

Precious objects of the Jacobite period

By Gordon Foster

There exists a vast array of Jacobite relics: many Scottish collections have pieces ranging from snuff boxes, quaichs, Jacobite glasses, portrait miniatures, medals, rings and of course locks of hair and fragments of Prince Charles Edward Stuart's plaid. The Jacobite souvenir industry in the early eighteenth century and later was big business.

There is no doubt about the Prince's generosity. His very first recorded act on landing safely at Loch Nan-uamh was to reward the captain of the Du Teillay, *Antoine Vincent Walsh, with a knighthood, together with a gold hilted sword and £2,000, a considerable sum in 1745.*

The early eighteenth century was the zenith of activity for Scottish silversmiths. There was a huge demand for all sorts of secular domestic plate and, of course, pistols, sword hilts, targes and other weapons were furbished with silver mounts. Many of the clan chiefs and officers in the Jacobite army carried such items. Prince Charles Edward, as we would expect, wore and carried the most fantastic Highland outfit and accoutrements. These were gifted to him in 1740 by James, 3rd Duke of Perth and included, along with Highland clothing, plaid, etc, a wonderful group of weapons and travelling canteen, now in the possession of the National Museums of Scotland. Prince Charles Edward's targe, or shield, is of typical construction – wood covered in pigskin with applied silver mounts of trophies of arms including Scottish pistols and broadswords. The centre has a grotesque Medusa mask, used in Greek mythology on warriors' shields for its petrifying power and also as a protective talisman.

The Prince's targe was left behind after Culloden but was rescued by the Jacobite colonel Ewan Macpherson of Cluny and retained in the Macpherson family until earlier this century. Also in the collection of the National Museums of Scotland is the Prince's basket-hilted broadsword, presented, too, by the 3rd Duke of Perth. The silver hilt is of exceptional quality; it was commissioned by the Duke in London from a leading silversmith, Charles Frederick Kandler.

Sadly there is no record of the silversmith's charge. Little is known of Kandler's history, despite the fact that he undertook many important commissions. It is still unknown whether there is a connection between him and the famous Meissen porcelain modeller of the same name. The late Norman Penzer, when researching the great wine cooler by Kandler in The Hermitage, St Petersburg, was unable despite considerable effort to discover anything about his origin. Suffice it to say that it is testimony to the high regard in which the Prince was held, that such an expensive commission was carried out.

The silver hilt is richly chased with similar decoration to the targe. It too was lost at Culloden and passed into the possession of the Duke of Cumberland. It remained in the royal collection until 1820, when George IV presented it to MacDonald of Clanranald.

A V B Norman has recently identified a silver-hilted sword from the collection of the Dukes of Gordon, which passed by marriage and descent to Brodie of Brodie, as a sword with cast decoration which is a closer match to the targe than the sword by Kandler. As two sets of Highland costume were made, we may see the Brodie sword as the companion to the targe at Warwick Castle.

But perhaps the quintessential piece of Jacobite silver is the unique silver gilt travelling canteen of Prince Charles Edward Stuart made in Edinburgh 1740-1 by Ebenezer Oliphant, possibly as a twenty-first birthday present from a dedicated Jacobite supporter, as yet unidentified.

The canteen comprises a set of two beakers, two knives, two forks and two spoons, a marrow scoop/spoon, a nutmeg grater/corkscrew, a salt box and dram dish, all housed in a finely chased outer case richly decorated with thistles and foliage – ideal accoutrements for a picnic for two! The dram dish is of interest: the design is French in origin, almost like a tastevin, so it may have been commissioned from France, possibly by the Prince's father James Francis Edward Stuart, 'The Old Pretender'. The canteen, like the targe and sword, fell into the hands of the Duke of Cumberland after Culloden and was presented to his aide-de-camp George Keppel, Lord Bury, later Earl of Albemarle. It remained in his family until it was sold in 1963. In 1984 it came up for sale again and with the help of various organisations was bought by the National Museums of Scotland. Another more functional silver gilt canteen used by the Prince is in the collections at Beaufort Castle.

SNUFF MULL CARRIED BY DAVID, LORD OGILVY DURING THE '45.

The French connection is of interest and three items in this exhibition are noteworthy in this respect. The French tumbler cup from the collection of Lord Airlie of Cortachy Castle is of typical 'Scottish' form. The base is engraved with various motifs and the side with the arms of Ogilvy. The Lochiel snuffbox has a French maker's mark although, again, it is Scottish in style.

But perhaps the most interesting is the small travelling writing set (écritoire) complete in its green stained fishskin case with silver rule, dividers, inkwell etc. It was given to Andrew Hay of Rannes by the Prince, whose original message to Andrew is on an ivory tablet within the case. These three pieces, amongst others, demonstrate the close links between Scottish and French silversmiths of the early eighteenth century.

The silver snuffbox engraved with Jacobite symbols is another piece of special interest in the exhibition. The symbols are well documented by Eric Delieb in his book Silver Boxes. *Delieb's conclusion is that the box was probably made in the Netherlands in the late seventeenth century, most probably for a fervent follower with strong Jacobite sympathies.*

Elaborate or simple, the precious objects in this Exhibition give an unusual perspective on the Jacobite story and Culloden in particular. Collectively they offer a fitting reminder of the extent of many adherents' support for the Jacobite cause.

THE EXHIBITS: SILVER AND GOLD

7:1 Oval Dutch Jacobite silver snuff box

The lid engraved with a symbolic series of Jacobite messages. A secret compartment within the lid with chased scene of dog gnawing at the bone of the enemy. *c*1700.

Dr J H Plum offers the following explanation of the emblems on the engraved lid:

The son (pun on sun) of Charles I, the figure at the top of the box. He is naked and therefore in heaven and a martyr. He will return or emerge (as the moon is emerging from the eclipse) from the Boscobel oak (the oak tree with the Welsh mountains behind, which was commonly used as a symbol for Charles II at the time of the Commonwealth) to his kingdom (indicated by the engraved city on the right) or from Breda, and restore the succession (the crown), royal authority (orb) and the church (mitre). He will bring peace (the sceptre laid across the sword), restore the coinage (the pieces of gold on the table), and hang (the halter) his enemies.

The rest of the story is told inside the chased lid. In a peaceful and plentiful countryside dogs are gnawing the bones of the king's enemies. The guineas on the table suggest that the box can be dated just after 1696, when the recoinage by William III's government brought about a chronic shortage of cash. This emblematic description of a Stuart restoration is probably cast in a historic form so that it could not be regarded as treasonable. It could be argued that it depicted only what had happened in 1660, although the implication, of course, is clear enough: what happened once might happen again. 3" x 2 1/4".

Lender: Gordon Foster.

7:2 Early 18th-century French silver tumbler cup

Engraved with the arms of Ogilvy. Marked with a crowned A and initials FD. *c*1730. 2 1/2" high x 2 1/8" diam.

This cup was carried at Culloden by the Jacobite Colonel David, Lord Ogilvy, commander of the Forfarshire Regiment, and a member of Prince Charles Edward Stuart's privy council. He escaped to Norway after the defeat at Culloden. The cup was taken from the dead body of the 11th Earl of Airlie at the battle of Diamond Hill, in South Africa, in June 1900.

Lender: The Earl of Airlie (Cortachy Castle).

7:3 Silver mounted cannonball

The silver band engraved *Ogilvy Culloden 16 April 1746*. 3 1/4" diam.

Lender: The Earl of Airlie.

David, Lord Ogilvy, by an unknown artist (c1750).

7:4 Scottish early 18th-century horn snuff mull with silver mounts

Engraved with the crest of Ogilvy and the motto *A Fin*. Carried by David, Lord Ogilvy during the '45. *c*1730. 4" long.

The word 'mull' is derived from 'mill': many snuff-boxes contained a small mill for grinding the snuff.

Lender: The Earl of Airlie.

7:5 Early 18th-century French écritoire

Complete with silver ink-well, the lid with wing-nut to retain it, fitted at one end of the green stained fishskin-covered case, and with silver spring catches. At the other end seven compartments contain, broken down into sections:

1 A silver rule with engraved floral decoration and engraved inch divisions. Engraved *Le Marie Fils, Paris* and on the reverse *Demey pied de Roy*.

2 A pair of steel-tipped silver compasses.

3 An octagonal pen and pencil holder with gold nib and silver and ebony shaft.

4 An ivory four-part writing tablet with silver pivot button, one tablet with faint writing in Prince Charles Edward Stuart's hand (authenticated by the British Museum in 1949): *This small swess is a present from Prince Charles as a memorandum of Rannes*. Hallmarked with an eagle head. *c*1740. 8" long.

Andrew Hay of Rannes was a major in Pitsligo's Horse, a small cavalry unit of local landowners and their retainers, formed by Alexander, 4th Lord Forbes of Pitsligo, Aberdeenshire. Hay was the first man to ride into Manchester at the head of Pitsligo's Horse. At 7' 2" tall, he was a very conspicuous fugitive after the defeat at Culloden. He escaped to France, was pardoned by George III in 1781, and died unmarried at Rannes on 29 August 1789, aged 76. His pardon is preserved at Leith Hall.

Lender: The National Trust for Scotland (Leith Hall).

Literature: Taylor, *Jacobites*.

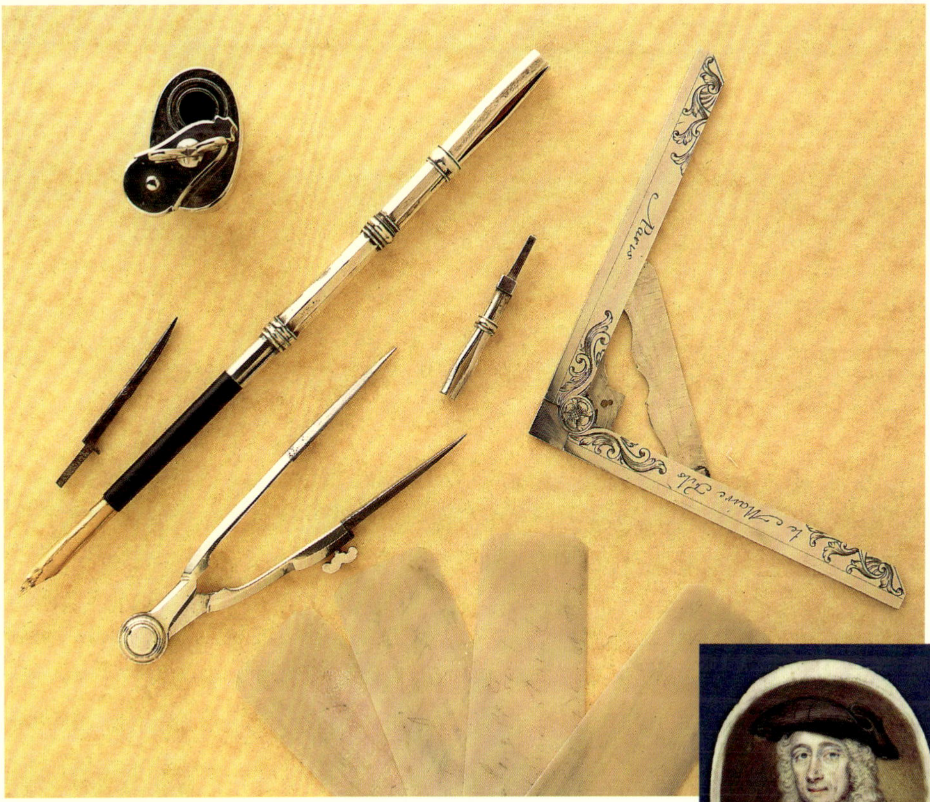

Andrew Hay of Rannes, by P Lens (c1750).

7:6 Scottish fruitwood quaich

With silver liner and rim engraved *Deoch slainnte nan gaidheal clann nam gael ri Guaillean a Chiele. In remembrance of Dugael Cameron, Culloden, 16 April 1746.* 5" wide.

Lender: Sir Donald Cameron of Lochiel.

7:7 *Early 18th-century French silver snuffbox*

The lid engraved with the coat-of-arms of Cameron of Lochiel, with the cypher of interlaced Ls. *c*1740. 3 1/2" wide x 2 1/4" high.

Lender: Sir Donald Cameron of Lochiel.

7:8 *Early 18th-century gold verge striking pocket watch*

By Conyers Dunlop, London, with enamelled dial and outer case.

Free of the Clockmakers Company 1733.

The watch of Alexander Irvine of Drum, who joined Prince Charles at Edinburgh, accompanying his friend Lord Pitsligo. He was present at Culloden and, escaping after the defeat, was for a time concealed at Drum Castle. Alexander Irvine was excepted from pardon in the Act of Indemnity, but he escaped forfeiture by the grand jury, who twice threw out bills for treason, returning an 'ignoramus' verdict in Edinburgh in October 1748, while Irvine was in Paris. He died at his seat of Drum on 9 February 1761. Although there is no record of this watch being carried into battle, it is likely, since such watches were in general everyday use at this time. 1 1/4 " diam.

Lender: The National Trust for Scotland (Drum Castle).

Literature: Taylor, *Jacobites.*

Alexander Irvine of Drum, by Cosmo Alexander.

7:9 *Gold locket with double-sided glass*

Containing hair from James III and VIII, his consort, Princess Clementina Sobieski, and his sons Prince Charles Edward and Henry, Duke of York. The gold rim is engraved *Francis Farquharson of Monaltrie, 1745.* The hair is held within gold initials surmounted by a gold crown. The reverse engraved *Hair of James (son of King James VII) of his consort and their sons Charles Edward and Henry. c*1745. 2" diam.

Known as Baron Bàn because of his fine bearing (*bàn* = handsome in Gaelic), Francis Farquharson of Monaltrie was captured after Culloden, sent to the Tower of London, sentenced to death, reprieved on the day of his execution and spent the next 16 years in captivity.

Lender: Captain Alwyne Compton Farquharson of Invercauld.

Francis Farquharson of Monaltrie, by an unknown artist (c1760).

7:10 Oval silver gilt snuffbox

Covered with varnished hardwood. A gilt oval on lid engraved WH. *c*1790. 3" long.

Lender: Logan Home, The National Trust for Scotland (Culloden).

7:12 Silver Gilt Travelling Canteen

Comprising a tapering oval beaker, double-lidded spice box, folding trifid spoon and fork, and a scroll-topped knife. The beaker and spice box are finely engraved with a horseman amongst scrolling foliage, the other pieces with scrolling foliage. With original shagreen-covered wooden truce, traditionally carved by Prince Charles Edward. Early 18th-century, struck with maker's mark F S (possibly for Francis Spilsbury).

Lender: Mrs Ann Gloag (Beaufort Castle).

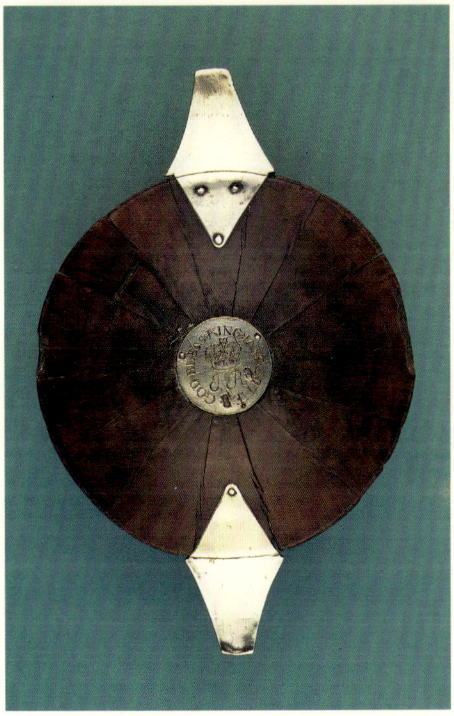

7:11 Silver mounted fruitwood quaich

The lug handles overlaid with silver, with a silver disc in the centre engraved *God bless King James 8*. *c*1730. 8" wide.

Lender: Logan Home, The National Trust for Scotland (Culloden).

THE EXHIBITS: TEXTILES

8:1 The Colour of the Stewarts of Appin Clan Regiment

This was carried at Culloden and was rescued by Donald Livingstone, saving it from the fate of the banners that were burned in Edinburgh by the public hangman. It was presented to the National Museums of Scotland by the Stewart Society. *c*1740. 48" x 42".

Lender: The Museum of Antiquities, Edinburgh.

Drambuie Ltd

Prince Charles Edward Stuart, by Cosmo Alexander (1752).

8:2 Piece of hard tartan

Said to have been worn by Prince Charles Edward Stuart at Moy Hall, February 1746.

Red/blue, 24" wide x !5" deep. This type of tartan with tightly spun yarn was used in the 18th century not only for dress but for bed-hangings. Given to Emily, Lady Glenlyon by Lady Mackintosh of Moy, passing to the 7th Duke of Atholl from Lady Charlotte Granville. *c*1745.

Lender: The Duke of Atholl (Blair Castle).

8:3 Piece of hard tartan

This small fragment of tartan is of similar texture to 8:2 and is traditionally a piece of cloth from the Prince's clothing. 9" wide x 4" deep.

Lender: The National Trust for Scotland (Brodie Castle).

8:4 *Piece of Garter ribbon*

A 4ft length of pale blue silk ribbon, stitched to an old label on which is handwritten in ink: *Ribbon worn by Prince Charles Edward Stuart in the year 1745, given by him to Miss Barbara Stuart and left by her to Charlotte Duchess of Richmond and Lennox, and left by Her Grace to Elizabeth, Duchess of Gordon.* *c*1740. 48" long, $3^{1}/_{4}$" wide.

The ribbon is thought to be the Ribbon of the Order of the Garter worn by the Prince and seen in many portraits of him. Duchess Charlotte (1768-1842) was the wife of Charles, 4th Duke of Richmond. Elizabeth (Brodie) (1794-1864), Duchess of Gordon, was the wife of George, 5th Duke of Gordon.

Lender: The National Trust for Scotland (Brodie Castle).

Literature: George Gordon, *The Last Dukes of Gordon and their Consorts*, Aberdeen, 1980.

8:5 *Piece of Garter ribbon*

An identical fragment of ribbon to 8:4 was given by the Prince to Lord Ogilvy. *c*1740. 4" x 2" framed.

Not illustrated.

Lender: The Earl of Airlie.

Lord George Murray, by an unknown artist (c1740)

8:6 *White cockade*

The Jacobite badge derived from the white rose. It was a length of white corded ribbon pleated into four folds and gathered into a bow by a short piece of ribbon stitched at the back. This cockade was worn in the bonnet of Lord George Murray. *c*1745. $1^{3}/_{4}$" wide.

Lender: The Duke of Atholl (Blair Castle).

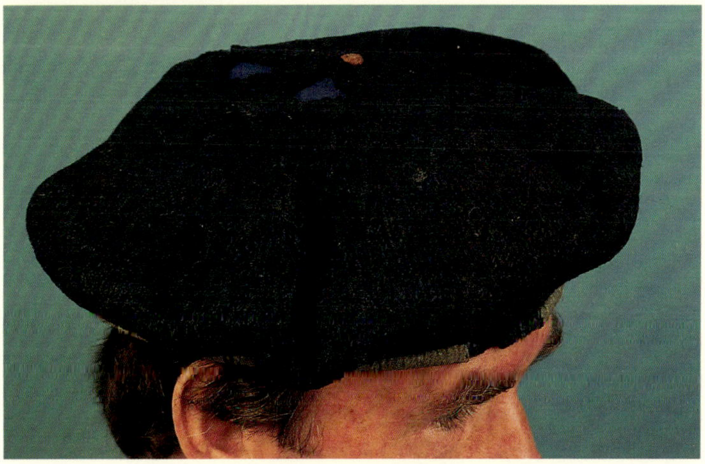

8:7 *Man's blue bonnet*

Said to have been worn by Prince Charles Edward Stuart, and left at Moy.

Felted knitting, with inner band of wool, covered with yellow corded silk ribbon. There are traces of ribbon hanging at the back. Some moth damage. 11" circ.

Lender: Mackintosh of Mackintosh, Moy Hall.

THE EXHIBITS: MISCELLANEOUS ARTICLES

9:1 Threipland medicine chest

A fully fitted mahogany case with various compartments containing a large selection of drugs and potions carried during the '45 by the Prince's chief medical officer, Sir Stewart Threipland. *c*1730. 10" x 10".

Lender: The Royal College of Physicians, Edinburgh.

Literature: R Girdwood, *The Lilly Lecture,* Royal College of Physicians, Edinburgh, 1979.

9:2 Early 18th-century leather, iron and brass bridle covered in faded maroon velvet

The bit with two cast brass rosettes, and decorated with five silk tassels. From the mount of the 4th Earl of Kilmarnock. *c*1740. 24" high.

William Boyd, 4th Earl of Kilmarnock, led Kilmarnock's Horse as a Jacobite colonel, although he came from a family of supporters of the House of Hanover. He was captured at the Battle of Culloden and executed in London.

Lender: The National Trust for Scotland (Culloden).

William Boyd, 4th Earl of Kilmarnock by an unknown artist

9:3 Early 18th-century three-legged cast-iron cooking pot with engraved brass plaque and detachable swing handle

The plaque reads: *Cooking pot used by Prince Charlie when living in the cave at Glendo, Glenmoriston during August 1746.* *c*1730. 18" high.

From John William O'Sullivan's narrative: 'They were not well arrived in the Cave, when they saw two detachments one at one side and one at the other side of the Glen. Those detachments drew nearer and nearer, the Prince thought he cou'd not escape them. Yt detachment yt was over against him past the torrent & drew very near the Cave. He propos'd to those peoples to march to them, & strive to make the best of their way, yt he'd answer to kill two, one with his Gun & the other with his pistol.'

Lender: Ian Grant of Glenmoriston.

9:4 Small early 18th-century copper kettle

Swing handle with the initials J C engraved on the top *c*1740. 7" high.

Known as Prince Charles Edward Stuart's campaign kettle.

Lender: The Duke of Buccleuch & Queensberry, KT (Drumlanrig Castle).

9:5 Brass-bound oak casket

Veneered in walnut, the brass mounts forming hinges shaped as fleurs-de-lis. The hasp is released by pushing down a brass button; this exposes an escutcheon with key slot. The lid and front of the casket can then be unlocked. Within the sides two iron bolts can be lowered by means of a T-shaped key, allowing the casket to be secured to a strong point. *c*1690. $12^{1}/_{2}$" long x 9" wide x 8" high.

Known as Prince Charles Edward Stuart's money box. The prince was at Drumlanrig on 22 December 1745 on his return from Carlisle and could have left the box and kettle as presents.

Lender: The Duke of Buccleuch & Queensberry, KT (Drumlanrig Castle).

9:6 Early 18th-century Scottish brass and leather sporran

Worn at Culloden by a member of the Atholl Brigade. 1730. 7" deep.

Lender: The Duke of Atholl (Blair Castle).

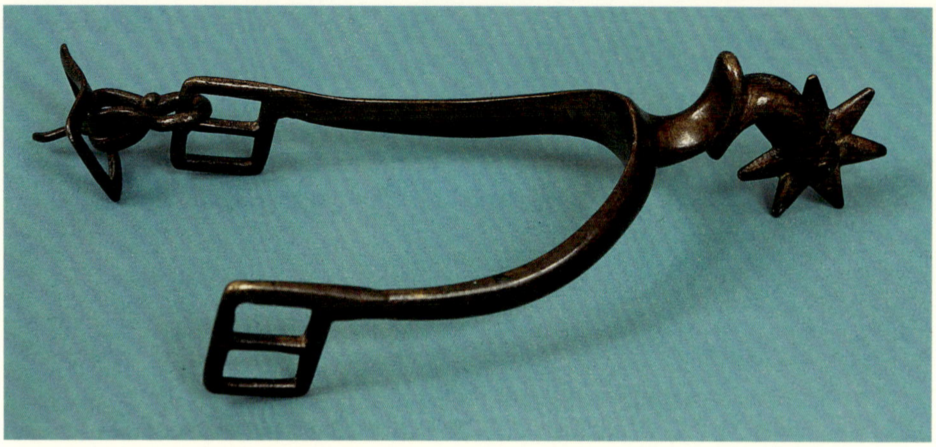

9:7 Eighteenth-century brass spur with eight-pointed star-shaped rowel

The strap buckle indicates that it was from the right boot. *c*1740. 7" x 3". Found on the field at Culloden.

Lender: The Museum of Antiquities, Edinburgh.

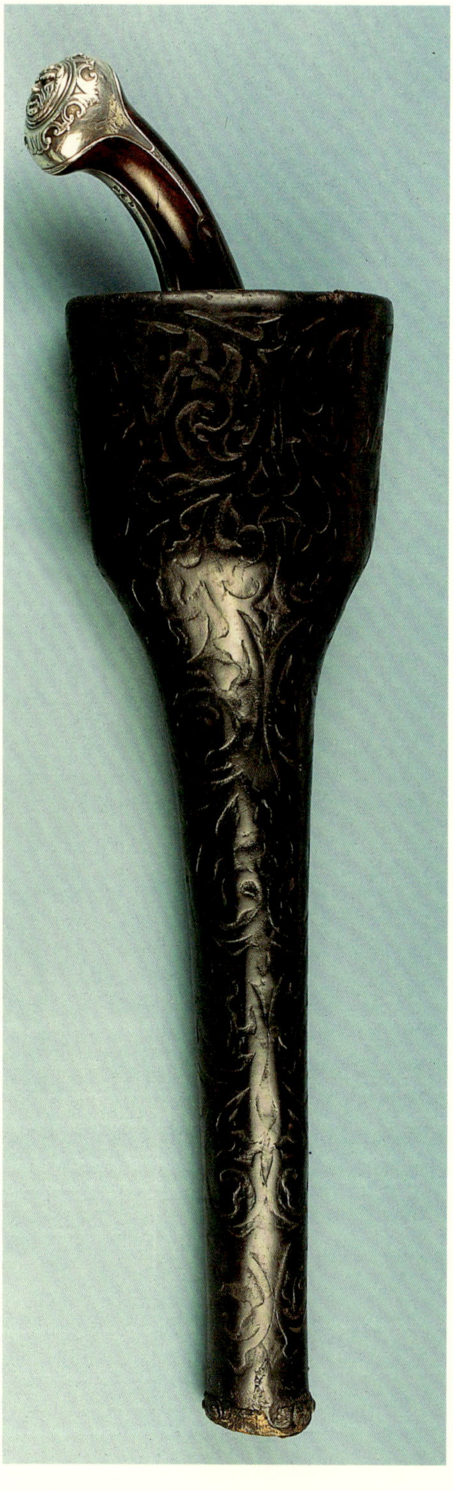

9:8 Late 17th-century carved wood, embossed leather-covered pistol holster

Holster pistols survive in large numbers, but holsters do not. They were normally made in pairs and were joined by a wide leather strap, which fitted over the neck of the horse just forward of the saddle. 20" high.

Lender: William Keith Neal Foundation.

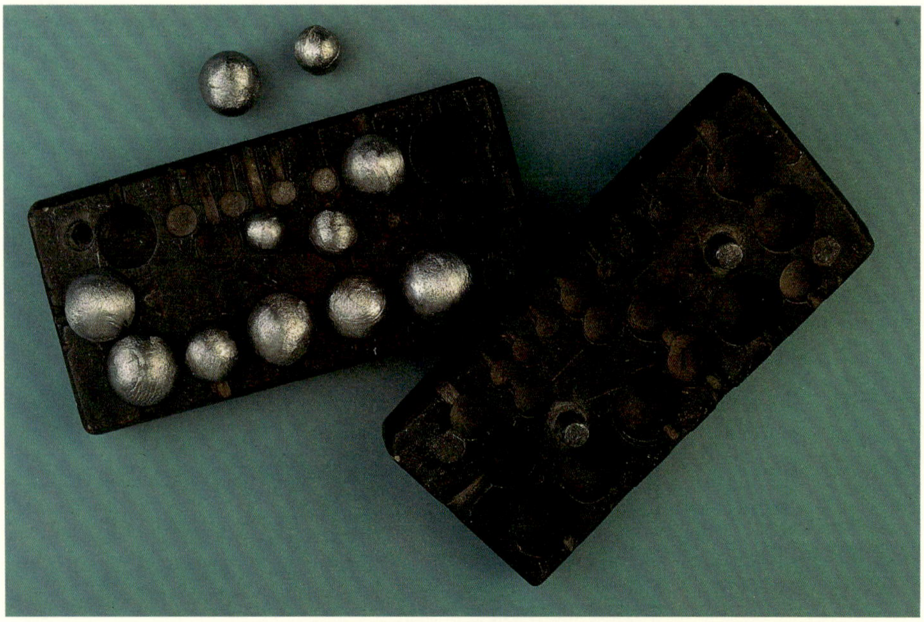

9:9 An 18th-century hardstone multi-bore bullet mould

With a capacity for producing 19 lead balls at each pouring. *c*1730. 8" long.

Lender: The National Trust for Scotland (Culloden).

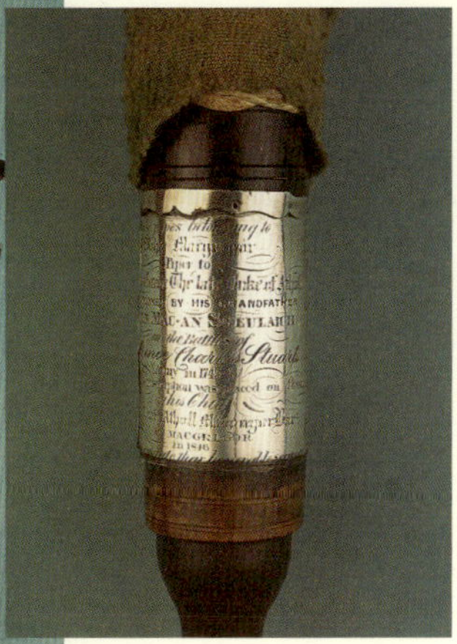

9:10 Set of early 18th-century Highland bagpipes

With chanter and two drones, mouth-blown. The chanter of silver-mounted hardwood, the tenor drone mounted with horn. The bag cover of green fringed felted cloth.

An engraved inscription on a silver plaque reads (in Gaelic and English): 'These pipes belonging to John Macgregor piper to His Grace the late Duke of Atholl were played by his grandfather John Mac-an Sgeulaich in the battles of Prince Charles Stuart's Army in 1745-6 and this inscription was placed on them by his chief Sir John Atholl Macgregor Bart in 1846 to commemorate their honourable service'.

Pipes were regarded by the British government as weapons of war.

Overall length 1'6".

Lender: The Duke of Atholl.

9:11 A set of early 18th-century Highland bagpipes

With chanter and two drones, mouth-blown. The chanter of laburnum wood, one ivory mount with EAML scratch-engraved on top surface. The bag covered in Mackenzie tartan.

Lender: Private collection.

9:12 Proclamation from Prince Charles Edward Stuart

Offering a reward of thirty thousand pounds sterling for the person of the Elector of Hanover.

This was 'Given in Our Camp at Kinlocheil, August the 22nd, 1745'.

Produced in retaliation for the reward of a similar amount for the capture of the Prince. 6 3/4" x 11".

Lender: John Kirk.

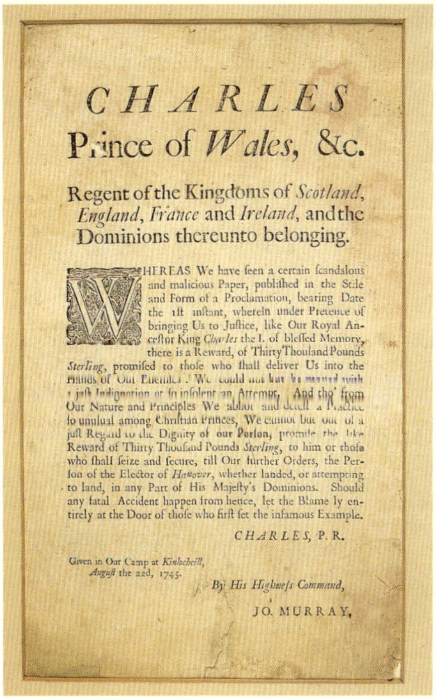

CHARLES
Prince of *Wales*, &c.

Regent of the Kingdoms of *Scotland*, *England*, *France* and *Ireland*, and the Dominions thereunto belonging.

WHEREAS We have ſeen a certain ſcandalous and malicious Paper, publiſhed in the Stile and Form of a Proclamation, bearing Date the 1ſt inſtant, wherein under Pretence of bringing Us to Juſtice, like Our Royal Anceſtor King *Charles* the I. of bleſſed Memory, there is a Reward, of Thirty Thouſand Pounds *Sterling*, promiſed to thoſe who ſhall deliver Us into the Hands of Our Enemies: We could not but be moved with a juſt Indignation at ſo inſolent an Attempt. And tho' from Our Nature and Principles We abhor and deteſt a Practice ſo unuſual among Chriſtian Princes, We cannot but out of a juſt Regard to the Dignity of our Perſon, promiſe the like Reward of Thirty Thouſand Pounds *Sterling*, to him or thoſe who ſhall ſeize and ſecure, till Our further Orders, the Perſon of the Elector of *Hanover*, whether landed, or attempting to land, in any Part of His Majeſty's Dominions. Should any fatal Accident happen from hence, let the Blame ly entirely at the Door of thoſe who firſt ſet the infamous Example.

CHARLES, P. R.

Given in Our Camp at *Kinlocheill*,
Auguſt the 22d, 1745.

By His Highneſs Command,

JO. MURRAY.

Scottish painting during the century of Jacobite exile 1688–1788

By James Holloway

The exile of King James VII and II at the end of the year 1688 signalled not merely the beginning of the long and ultimately ill-fated Jacobite cause, but the collapse of the brief flowering of the arts which had been nurtured by the king and centred on the Palace of Holyroodhouse in Edinburgh. As an important part of Stuart political policy, the rambling old tower house at the foot of the Canongate was transformed under James's elder brother, King Charles II, into a modern baroque palace, designed to be an expression in stone of the king's power and presence in Scotland. Craftsmen were brought from all over northern Europe to work on the project. Holyroodhouse, when completed, was the focus once more of a royal court centred on James, High Commissioner for Scotland, and his wife Maria d'Este.

The architect of the new palace and the man who co-ordinated the extensive building and decorative works, Sir William Bruce, never recovered from the exile of the House of Stuart. Nor did the painter John Michael Wright, who had had many royal commissions from both Charles and James. As a contemporary recorded: 'For his royal master being now gone, he soon found that he had lost an extraordinary friend, and 'tis therefore from that time that he dated his own ruin'.

The arrival on the thrones of England and Scotland of William of Orange in 1689 brought new men to power. Those men, and especially their wives, demanded new artists. One such was John de Medina. As his name suggests, he was of Spanish descent but he had been born in Brussels and had moved to London in 1686 seeking work. He was successful and had come to the attention of two of King William's most loyal Scottish supporters, the Earl of Melville and his son the Earl of Leven. They sat to Medina in London and their portraits were despatched north to their families in Scotland.

Medina painted in an up-to-date baroque style and when Lady Melville and her daughter-in-law saw his work they realised its superiority over the much more primitive portraits which were all they were able to commission in Scotland. Lord Melville and Lord Leven were urged to bring Medina to Edinburgh, something to which, initially, the artist was understandably reluctant to agree. However, the promise of much business persuaded Medina to pay a brief visit to Edinburgh where, probably much to his surprise, he prospered. He never returned to London, but spent the rest of his life in the city, where he was knighted and died a rich man.

Medina's studio was in the Canongate, not far from the Palace of Holyroodhouse, by then deserted. It was at that studio that Medina's successor was trained. William Aikman

ARCHIBALD, 1ST DUKE OF ARGYLL, WITH HIS SONS JOHN AND ARCHIBALD, BY JOHN DE MEDINA.

had been destined by his well-connected relations for the law or for a career in busines. Instead, he chose to become an artist and managed to finance his training by selling his family estate in Angus. He travelled to Italy and to the Eastern Mediterranean, and in London was part of the circle of that leader of taste, Lord Burlington. He was a close friend of the poet Alexander Pope. Aikman returned to Edinburgh on Medina's death in 1710 and soon dominated the Scottish portrait business. His paintings differ from his master's in mood and colour: where Medina's portraits were resonant and confidently conceived, Aikman's are more reticent and quieter in colour, as if in music there had been a change from a major to a minor key. One of Aikman's most important patrons was John, 2nd Duke of Argyll, the head of Clan Campbell, a distinguished soldier and one of the leading political figures of the recently United Kingdom. The duke's patronage was of enormous importance to the artist: it brought him commissions not only from the duke's immediate family but from his kinsmen and numerous political appointees. It was the duke who persuaded Aikman to try his luck in London – sensible advice, since the dissolution of the Scottish parliament in 1707 had relegated Edinburgh to the status of a provincial city. Scotsmen and women who wanted to play a part on a national stage now needed to be in London. While Aikman in Edinburgh was able to make a comfortable living, Aikman in London could hope for much more. The fact that he succeeded – his clients included the royal family and the Prime Minister – was due not only to his own ability but to Campbell patronage.

Drambuie Ltd

PRINCE CHARLES EDWARD STUART, BY COSMO ALEXANDER (1752).

The Earl of Mar had led the Jacobite Rising of 1715 and had fought against Aikman's patron, the Duke of Argyll, at the Battle of Sheriffmuir. After the failure of that rising the talented Lord Mar fled to the Continent and joined the Stuart royal family in exile in Italy.

John Alexander, an artist from Aberdeen, was there painting for the Jacobite court. Two pictures which Alexander painted for Lord Mar, *Perseus and Andromeda* and *Perseus cutting off Medusa's head*, were chosen, in the artist's words, 'because I found them applicable to Your Grace in the last conjuncture you had in Scotland'. Alexander was also keen to illustrate episodes from the life of Mary, Queen of Scots. Once again, the Roman Catholic and Jacobite artist found a parallel between the past and the present. Mary's harsh treatment at the hands of the English Queen Elizabeth was compared with the contemporary misfortunes of the Stuarts, caused by the House of Hanover.

Major David Tulloch of Dunbennan, by Cosmo Alexander (c1740).

Another Jacobite grandee to retire to Italy after the Battle of Sheriffmuir was the Duke of Gordon. He was in Florence in 1717, visiting his friend the Duke of Tuscany. It is likely that the Scottish duke encouraged Alexander to dedicate his set of engravings after paintings by Raphael to Duke Cosimo III de' Medici. Back in Scotland the Duke of Gordon had a much more ambitious project for the artist – to decorate the ceiling over the main staircase at Gordon Castle. By 1720 John Alexander had completed his oil sketch for the 20ft-square ceiling. It showed *The Rape of Proserpine*, the composition of which was loosely based on a ceiling painting in the Palazzo Barberini in Rome which had been painted by Alexander's Italian master Giuseppe Chiari.

John Alexander also painted three large views of Rome for the castle and portraits of the duke's Gordon kinsmen. Like virtually every other early eighteenth-century Scottish artist, he made his living through portrait painting. With family connections in Aberdeenshire, John Alexander took a large share of business in the north-east. When his son Cosmo grew old enough to paint he continued in his father's linear style, softening it somewhat for the taste of the mid-century.

Cosmo Alexander shared his father's religious and political sympathies. During the second great Jacobite Rising, in 1745, he took up arms for Prince Charles Edward Stuart. After its collapse, he fled to Rome as his father had done thirty years earlier, to find patrons amongst the exiled Scottish community in the city. Lesser painters were also associated with Jacobite families. One was William Robertson, who was particularly favoured by the predominantly Episcopalian and Jacobite gentry in Angus and Perthshire.

Allan Ramsay's poet father had Jacobite sympathies which at the start of his career may have been shared by his ambitious and talented son. Allan Ramsay junior was the outstanding Scottish painter of the eighteenth century, an artist who developed into one of the finest in Europe. He was trained in Edinburgh and would almost certainly have worked alongside his father's close friend William Aikman had the latter not died prematurely. Aikman, however, remained a role model for the young artist; a gentleman born and bred, who had pursued a successful career in London. It was probably Aikman's example that determined Ramsay to visit Italy for a long period of study. It was certainly his father's connections which helped finance him.

Ashmolean Museum.

Flora MacDonald, by Allan Ramsay (c1749).

As well as hard work in the teaching academies and artists' studios of Rome and hours of laborious work copying the old masters in palaces and churches, Ramsay found time for a social life. Many of his friends were drawn from the circle of Jacobite exiles in the city. One afternoon Ramsay was introduced to the young Stuart princes, Charles and Henry, at the Villa Ludovisi. Afterwards he stayed on to watch them shoot blackbirds in the villa gardens. The artist was a guest at the grand ball, held at the Corsini Palace on New Year's Eve 1736, to celebrate Bonnie Prince Charlie's sixteenth birthday. Years later he had another, less pleasant encounter with the House of Stuart when, in 1745, Jacobite troops under the command of Cameron of Lochiel were engaged in a skirmish outside his studio on Edinburgh's Castlehill.

On his return from Italy it was Campbell patronage, which had been of such benefit to Aikman a generation earlier, that helped Ramsay further his career. John, 2nd Duke sat to him in 1749 at a time when the young artist probably needed his support much more than the Duke another portrait. Ducal approbation led to further Campbell commissions and Ramsay, newly settled in London, soon had the lion's share of the Scottish business in the capital, as well as important portraits to paint for English clients. After Duke John's death in 1743 his brother Archibald sat to Ramsay and continued to use him for a number of formal portraits which in turn were engraved and copied.

George III as Prince of Wales, by Allan Ramsay.

Of course it was Ramsay's innate talent that made him a great painter, but in the competitive world in which he operated active support from his father and from the influential Campbells was necessary too. In the end it was the Hanoverian royal family who were his greatest patrons. Through the influence of the Earl of Bute, the nephew and protégé of the two Dukes of Argyll, Ramsay was introduced to the Prince of Wales who, on his accession to the throne in 1760 as King George III, employed Ramsay as his official painter. When one of the court was foolhardy enough to suggest that the king might care to sit to the famous English painter, Joshua Reynolds, George tartly replied: 'Mr Ramsay is my painter, my Lord'. Indeed, Ramsay served his royal patrons well, providing them with a succession of grand and sensitive state portraits for public display while painting more intimate portraits for the family themselves. Ramsay died in 1784. Four years later Bonnie Prince Charlie died and with him any lingering hopes the remaining, ageing Jacobite adherents had of the restoration of the royal House of Stuart.

GLOSSARY

SWORDS

Arms of the hilt The two half-circular guards forward of the quillons on a rapier or small-sword.

Associated Term used by modern writers of parts of a weapon which are thought not to be original.

Backsword Sword with a straight one-edged blade (Gaelic, *claidheamh cùil*).

Ballock-knife or dagger Weapon with phallus-like haft.

Basket hilt A hilt enclosing the hand, constructed of bars and broad plates (Gaelic, *caenn-aisneach*).

Blueing The surface colouring of steel either by mechanical or chemical means.

Boat-shell hilt A small sword with a heart-shaped guard in front of the hand.

Broadsword A sword with a broad, straight two-edged blade (Gaelic, *claidheamh mòr* or *claidheamh leathann*).

Byknife Knife fitted in the sheath of a dirk.

Chape See crampet.

Claymore (Gaelic, *claidheamh mòr* = great sword) The basket-hilted Highland broad-sword.

Crampet (Gaelic, *crambait*) Metal mount on the point of the scabbard, equivalent to the English 'chape'.

Cross hilt The simplest form of hilt with a guard consisting only of a single bar (the quillons).

Cuttoe 18th-century English term for a hanger, derived from the French *couteau-de-chasse* (hunting knife).

Damascening The technique of decorating steel with precious metal. Two forms exist: in 'true' damascening, the design is cut into the surface and the gold or silver is secured in V-shaped grooves by hammering. In counterfeit-damascening, the commoner method, the surface of the steel is roughened with a file and the precious metal secured by hammering it into the slight grooves or ridges produced in this way.

Dirk A Scottish dagger, a late form of the ballock knife (Gaelic, *biodag*).

False edge The sharpened part near the point on the back of some one-edged blades.

Ferrule A band (often in the form of a Turk's-head knot) around each end of the grip to secure the binding.

Frog An attachment for carrying a sword or bayonet from a waist-belt or baldrick.

Fuller Groove in the blade of a sword or dagger which lightened it without weakening it.

Garniture A set of two or more objects made to match each other.

Grip The part of the hilt which acts as the 'handle'.

Haft The wooden shaft of a staff weapon. The hilt of a dagger.

Hanger A short sword with a straight, or slightly curved, one-edged blade.

Hilt The part of a sword comprising pommel, grip and guard.

Jacobite sword blades Blades etched with inscriptions and devices supporting James VIII and III (1688-1766). Some call for the repeal of the Act of Union (1707) between the parliaments of Scotland and England and proclaim him as James VIII. Others proclaim him as James III and were therefore intended for English Jacobites.

Japanning A process of coating with black paint, usually decorated with gold or coloured paint.

Langets Small finger-like projections from the centre of the quillons flanking the blade.

Mounts Metal parts of a scabbard or sheath; the mouth-piece, hook or hooks, and crampet.

Mouth-piece Mount at the top of the scabbard, the equivalent of the English 'locket'.

One-edged blade A sword or knife blade with one edge only.

Pike Long spear (up to 22ft long), employed by armoured infantrymen (pikemen) to protect the musketeers from cavalry attack.

Pommel Knob at the end of a sword or dagger hilt furthest from the blade. It counter-balances the weight of the blade.

Quillon-block The reinforced centre of the quillons which is pierced for the tang of the blade to pass through.

Quillon dagger Modern term for a cross-hilted dagger. The most common of all dagger hilts, in use from the Middle Ages onwards.

Quillons The cross-guard on a sword hilt. On a basket hilt these form the transverse bar supporting the other guards.

Ricasso The part of the blade near the hilt, usually only a few inches long, which is of rectangular cross-section.

Russeting The colouring of steel by means of a corrosive.

Scabbard Protective cover for a sword blade, usually made of wood and covered with leather or, in the case of Highland and military swords, made of leather only (Gaelic, *truaill*). It has a metal crampet at the tip, one or two suspension-hooks and sometimes a metal mouth-piece.

Shell or shell-guard A plate supported on the centre of the quillons to protect the hand.

Side-ring The ring-guard supported on the centre of the quillons, usually at right angles to the plane of the blade, to protect the hand.

Skean dhu (Gaelic,*sgian dubh* = black knife) A Highlander's small knife worn in the top of his stocking.

Small-sword The lighter, more manageable sword developed in the middle years of the 17th century as a court sword and still used as such (Gaelic, *claidheamh caol*).

Staff weapon The term used to describe weapons fitted on a staff or pole.

Sword-knot A wrist cord or strap attached to a sword hilt to prevent the sword from being lost in action.

Tang The narrow continuation of the blade which fits through the hilt and grip.

Targe (Gaelic, *targaid*) The round shield or target used by the Highlanders. They are usually of two-ply wood, covered on the front with dressed leather and on the back with the skin of cattle, deer or goat, still with the hair. The outer surface is decorated with tooling, and dome-headed nails and bosses.

Two-edged blade A blade sharpened along both edges.

Two-handed sword Sword with a long grip to be wielded with both hands (Gaelic, *claidheamh dà làimh*).

Wolf mark The mark of the bladesmiths of Passau and later of Solingen, Germany.

FIREARMS

Barrel The tube which directs the missile: from early cannon.

Bayonet A dagger for attaching to a gun barrel, named after the blade-producing centre of Bayonne, south-west France, and probably first used for hunting in the 16th and 17th centuries. By the last quarter of the 17th century most European armies had equipped their troops with bayonets so they could defend themselves after firing. The early plug bayonet had a tapered handle which fitted into the gun muzzle: this was soon replaced by the socket bayonet which fitted over the barrel, enabling the gun to fire when the bayonet was attached.

Blunderbuss A short heavy weapon for scattering shot at close range.

Bore The internal diameter of the barrel.

Carbine A cavalry firearm, shorter than an infantry musket.

Carbine bore A bore somewhat smaller than a musket bore (about $^{13}/_{20}$").

Cartridge Originally a paper bag holding bullet and charge for a muzzle-loader, the paper serving as wad. Now a complete primed charge in a brass or cardboard-brass case, for breech.

Chasing A method of decorating metal, in firearms usually called chiselling (*qv*).

Chiselling Cutting metal with specially hardened tools to leave a pattern in relief; a high point of the art, favoured for 'best' weapons in the 16th and 17th centuries, gradually superseded by engraving.

Cock An arm with jaws to hold match, pyrites or flint in early weapons. Half-cock: a partly-raised position from which the cock cannot be released; used also of hammer guns similarly set. To 'go off at half-cock' means to discharge accidentally. Full-cock: fully prepared for firing on the pressure of the trigger. To cock: to set at full-cock.

Engraving Incising metal by means of a hard sharp tool called a graver, capable in skilled hands of producing very delicate patterning, monograms, coats-of-arms etc.

Guard Part of a firearm not essential for its use but for safety; eg trigger-guard. Also, in breech-loading sporting guns, the detachable piece forward of the lock, below, which limits the opening of the gun when loading, and contains the ejector mechanism.

Gunpowder A mixture of saltpetre, sulphur and charcoal.

Gunmaker The maker of firearms.

Inlay Decorative materials let into parts of the gun, as ivory inlays in stocks in the 16th and 17th centuries and wire inlays in pistol-butts in the 18th century.

Lock the mechanism attached to the stock, which fires the charge in the barrel. The phrase 'lock, stock and barrel', means the whole thing complete. It was at one time usual for the lock, the stock and the barrel to be made by different specialists.

Mainspring The powerful leaf spring that operates the cock or hammer. Also applied to the spiral spring of a bolt-action firing-pin.

Musket A smooth-bore heavy shoulder-piece, the main infantry weapon for centuries. Fired by match, wheel or flint. In the 16th and early 17th centuries very long and heavy, nearly 5' long in the barrel; reducing by successive stages to 3'3" long during the Napoleonic Wars.

Musketry The art of shooting with musket or rifle; also, the organised fire from a formation of musketeers.

Pan In early weapons, an indentation on top of the barrel, above the touch-hole; later, a pan built on the side of the barrel and connecting with the touch-hole. The receptacle for the priming. A 'flash in the pan' results from igniting the priming without firing the effective charge – hence its figurative use.

Pan-cover A cover for the pan in early weapons, superseded by the steel or frizzen (*qv*).

Prime To fill the pan with gunpowder.

Priming The gunpowder in the pan, usually of a finer grain than the main charge.

Rifle A musket with a rifled barrel.

Rifling The spiral grooving inside the barrel of a rifle that grips the bullet and rotates it as it passes up the barrel.

Safety-catch A catch which, when applied, makes the weapon safe from accidental discharge, either by positively locking the hammer or firing-pin or by locking the trigger.

Sear The pawl or pin that holds the tumbler and hammer in the cocked position, until released by pressing the trigger.

Sear spring The light spring that holds the sear in position; its resistance to the trigger pressure determines the weight of the 'pull'.

Steel or **frizzen** The striking-plate of a flintlock, combined with the pan-cover.

Stock The whole of the wooden part of a firearm. 'Butt' is used of that part of the stock which is behind the lock.

Tang A tongue of metal, a prolongation of a larger object, for fixing purposes.

Touch-hole The small hole which when filled with powder connects the priming in the pan with the charge in the barrel. In the earliest firearms the hole was 'touched' with a hot iron.

Tower The Tower of London, formerly the national arsenal. Most early military weapons have the word 'Tower' stamped or engraved on the lock-plate or the tang of the barrel.

Trigger The small lever which is pressed to disengage the sear from the tumbler and so fire the weapon.

Turn-off pistol A pistol having the barrel made to screw off for loading; also called Queen Anne pistol and screw pistol.

View To examine a firearm with great care in every part, to ascertain that there is no apparent defect before it goes to proof.

View mark After viewing, if passed, the viewer stamps the barrel with the View Mark, usually 'V' with crown or crossed keys above it.

BIBLIOGRAPHY

J Anderson & J Drummond, *Ancient Scottish Weapons*, 1881.

L G Boccia & E T Coelho, *Armi Bianche Italiane*, Milan, 1975.

D H Caldwell (ed), *Scottish Weapons and Fortifications, 1100-1800*, Edinburgh, 1981.

Lord Archibald Campbell, *Highland Dress, Arms and Ornament*, London, 1899.

Cumberland Papers, Royal Archives, Windsor Castle.

J T Dunbar, *History of Highland Dress*, Edinburgh, 1962.

Sir James Fergusson of Kilkerran, *Argyll in the Forty-Five*, London, 1951.

I Finlay, *Scottish Gold and Silver Work*, 1st edition, London, 1956.

I Finlay, *Scottish Gold and Silver Work*, 2nd edition, Stevenage, 1991.

I Finlay, 'Highland Weapons at the Royal Academy', in *Connoisseur*, CIII, 1939.

A G Grimwade, *London Goldsmiths*, 1697-1837, London, 1976.

C Hesketh, *Tartans*, London, 1961.

I E James, *The Goldsmiths of Aberdeen*, Aberdeen, 1981.

Sir Guy Laking, *The Armoury of Windsor Castle*, London, 1904.

Sir Guy Laking, *A Record of European Arms and Armour* , II, London, 1920.

P J Lankester, 'Notes on some Scottish silver-hilted swords', *Journal of the Arms and Armour Society*, XIV, No.5, 1994.

J MacKenzie, *The Dewar Manuscript*, Glasgow, 1963.

Sir James Mann, *European Arms and Armour*, London, 1962.

A E H Miller & N P Dawnay, *Military Drawings and Paintings in the Royal Collection*, London, 1970.

R W Munro, *Highland Clans and Tartans*, London, 1977.

W Keith Neal and D H L Back, *British Gunmakers Messrs Griffin, Tow and W Bailes, 1740-90*, Norwich, 1989.

W Keith Neal and D H L Back, *British Gunmakers: their tradecards, cases and equipment*, Warminster, 1980.

W Keith Neal & D H L Back, *Great British Gunmakers 1540-1740,* Norwich, 1984.

W Keith Neal and D H L Back, *Great British Gunmakers 1740-90*, London, 1975.

A V B Norman, in *Boughton House; the English Versailles*, ed T Murdoch, London, 1992.

A V B Norman, 'Early military dirks in the Scottish United Services Museum, Edinburgh,' *Journal of the Arms and Armour Society*, Vol IV No 1, 1968.

A V B Norman, 'The John Simpsons of Glasgow', *Despatch*, (Journal of the Scottish Military Collectors Society), No13, (spring 1993).

A O'Connor & D V Clarke, *From the Stone Age to the 'Forty-Five*, Edinburgh, 1983.

J Paton (ed), *Scottish National Memorials* (catalogue of exhibition at Bishop's Castle), Glasgow, 1888.

I Pickford (ed), *Jackson's Silver and Gold Marks of England, Scotland and Ireland*, Woodbridge, Suffolk, 1989.

W Reid, 'A rare Scottish silver-hilted hanger in an important loan exhibition', in *Connoisseur*, CLII, 1963.

W Reid, 'Walter Allan, Armourer in Stirling', in *Scottish Art Review*, IX, No 1, 1963.

C R Rolland, 'Observations on the Dating of Scottish Basket Hilted Swords', in *Souvenir of the Seventh Park Lane Arms Fair*, London 1990.

W M Schmid, 'Passauer Waffenwesen', *Zeitschrift für Historische Waffenkunde*, VIII, 1918-20.

H Schneider, *Waffen im Schweizerischen Landesmuseum*; *Grifwaffen* 1, Zurich, 1980.

R L Scott, *Catalogue of the Collection of European Arms and Armour formed at Greenock*, Glasgow, 1924.

K A Steer & J W M Bannerman, *Late Medieval Monumental Sculpture in the West Highlands*, Edinburgh, 1977.

A & H Taylor, *Jacobites of Aberdeenshire & Banffshire in the '45*, Aberdeen, 1928.

A & H Taylor, *1745 and After*, London, 1938.

C Trenchard, 'Jacobite Sword Blades: a Record of all the Examples believed to be Extant', Pt I, *Antique Collector*, VII, February 1936.

J M Wallace, *Scottish Swords and Dirks*, London, 1970.

Wallace Collection Catalogues: *European Arms and Armour Supplement*, London, 1986.

A Weyersberg, *Solinger Schwertschmiede des 16. und 17. Jahrhunderts und ihre Erzeugnisse*, Solingen, 1926.

C E Whitelaw, *Catalogue of the Collection of Captain N R Colville*, undated and unpublished, in the Museum of Antiquities, Edinburgh.

C E Whitelaw, *Scottish Arms Makers*, London, 1977.

C E Whitelaw, 'Notes on swords with signed hilts by Glasgow and Stirling makers', in *Transactions of the Glasgow Archaeological Society*, N S VIII, pt 4 (supplement), 1934.

R C Woosnam-Savage, 'Scottish Long Guns in Scotland's Public Collections', in *Park Lane Arms Fair (tenth catalogue).*

R C Woosnam-Savage and C Blair, *Scottish Firearms*, Canadian Museum Restoration Service, 1995.

Printed in Scotland

P1746/14601. JTCP. 10M – 2/96.